THE INDIAN CONCH

THE INDIAN CONCH:

AND ITS RELATION TO HINDU LIFE AND RELIGION

JAMES HORNELL

GYAN

Published by

Gyan Publishing House
5, Ansari Road
Daryaganj, New Delhi-110002
Phone: 011-47034999, 9811692060
E-mail: books@gyanbooks.com

Distribution Network
gyanbooks.com
India, USA, Canada, UK, Australia

ISBN: 978-93-7014-167-4 (PB)

First Published, 1915

2nd Impression 2025

Printed at: Gyan Press, Delhi.

THE INDIAN CONCH
Author: JAMES HORNELL

THE INDIAN CONCH

AND ITS RELATION TO HINDU LIFE AND RELIGION

BY

JAMES HORNELL, F.L.S.

Marine Assistant, Department of Fisheries, Madras, and formerly Marine Biologist to the Government of Ceylon

1915

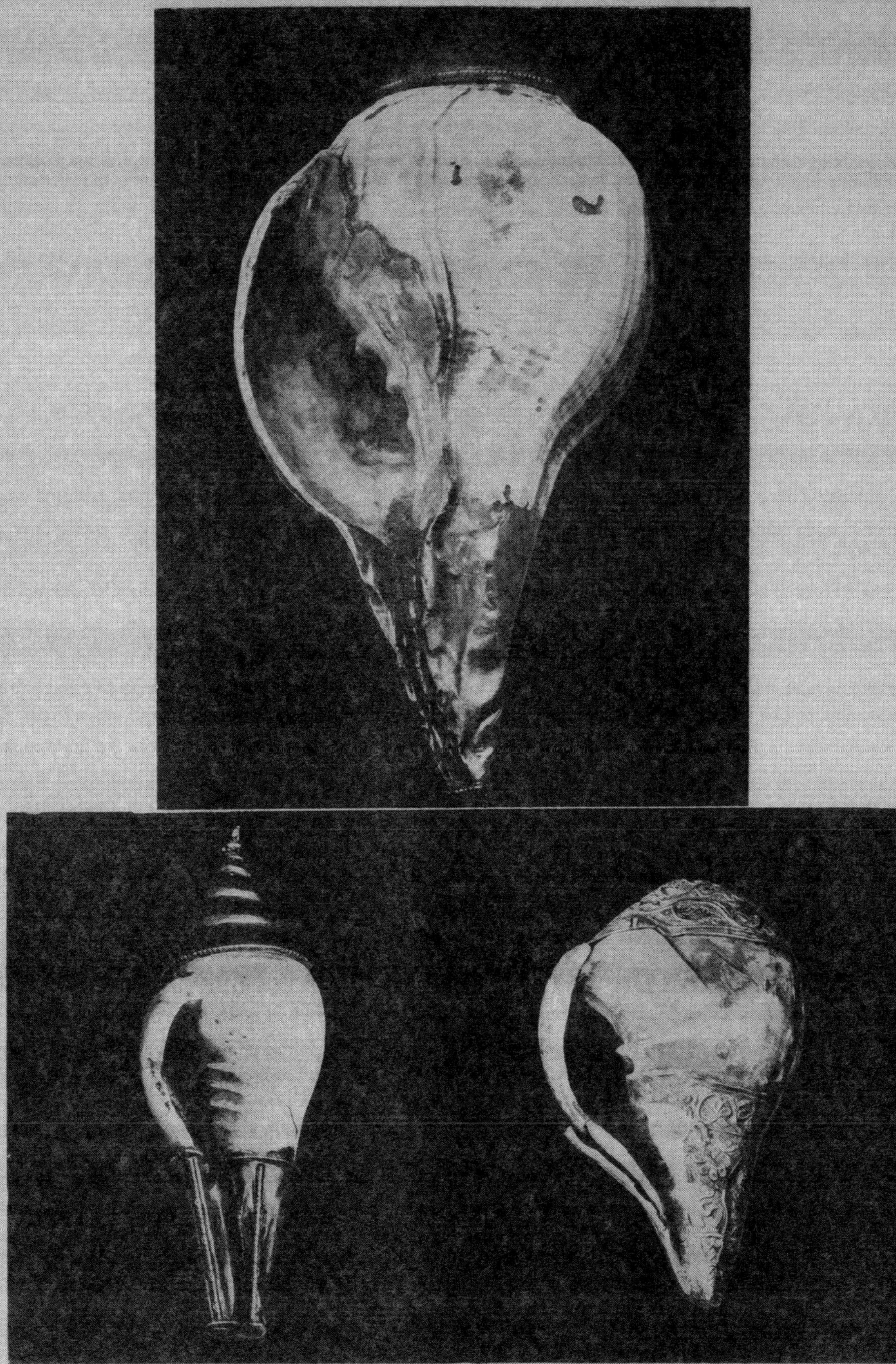

[Photographed by Vividha Kala Mandir, Baroda.

Figs. 1, 2 and 3.—Sinistral chanks respectively in the Satya Bhamaji, Shank Narayan and Lakshmi Temples, Bet, Kathiawar.

THE INDIAN CONCH

(TURBINELLA PYRUM, *LINN.*)

AND ITS RELATION TO HINDU LIFE AND RELIGION

BY

JAMES HORNELL, F.L.S.,

Marine Assistant, Department of Fisheries, Madras, and formerly Marine Biologist to the Government of Ceylon

[WITH SEVEN PLATES AND TWO TEXT-FIGURES]

INTRODUCTORY

To all Hindus the important position occupied by the Sacred Conch (*Turbinella pyrum*, Linn.), the *Sankha* of Sanscrit literature and the *Sanku* or *Chanku* of Tamil speech, in their religion is a commonplace of everyday knowledge; few, however, are aware of the intimate relationship it bears to a hundred common incidents in the ordinary life of the people in many localities and among widely sundered races, tribes, and castes. In the following pages an attempt will be made to survey this little known by-way in the life and history of the Indian world, to show how superstition looks upon the Sankha as an amulet against the powers of evil, how this belief is among the oldest and most tenaciously held by Animist and Hindu, by Muhammadan and by Buddhist; to indicate the way this belief has brought the shell into prominence in the Hindu religion, and to detail how it subserves as well, a hundred different uses in the daily lives of millions of Indians—how it is associated with infancy, marriage and death, and finally how its employment in the form of ornamental bangles was once the subject of an important industry in several widely separated parts of India, prominent being Kathiawar and Gujarat where to-day all memory of it has vanished.

In connection with this latter point I trust that the attention now drawn to it, may result in the revival in Kathiawar of an industry that has more good things than usual in its favour if we consider other aims than that of mere money-making; no objects manufactured in India are more artistic and pleasing than the handsome milk-white bangles made in Dacca workshops for the ladies of Bengal.

In the course of collecting the materials for this essay, difficult problems have taken form. Some we can solve, but others remain obscure; among the latter may be mentioned the unknown cause for the cessation and disappearance of the chank bangle industry in Kathiawar, Gujarat and the Deccan, and the question whether the use of chank bangles among a few sections of several castes in South India is in the nature of a survival of a once universal custom.

Another point to which I wish to draw attention is the bearing upon the antiquity of trade relations between India and the Persian Gulf in the recognition I made last year of several exhibits in the Louvre as consisting of objects carved from the shell of the Indian conch. True it is that they go back only some 500 years B.C. but it is something definitely accomplished when we can say with certainty that at this date we have positive evidence of the employment of the Indian chank, probably in religious service, in one of the great capitals of the Achæmenid dynasty of Persia. An examination of remains from Babylonian and Assyrian sites with a view to discover articles cut from this shell might well have profitable and important historical results.

I am well aware of the many lacunæ in the story I offer, particularly in regard to ancient references to the Sankha preserved in the Sanscrit classics; there may also be many valuable passages in ancient Gujarati works; these were sealed books to me and I can but hope that others with the necessary qualifications may make good what is wanting in the present account.

I

LIFE-HISTORY AND LOCAL RACES

THE Indian Conch, *Turbinella pyrum*, Linn., is a handsome gastropod mollusc found in Indian waters in large numbers in comparatively shallow water. Its geographical distribution is peculiar; on the west coast of India large numbers are fished off the Kathiawar coast, but southward of this, we find no trace of the chank till we reach the southern coastline of Travancore where this shell again appears and forms the object of a small fishery. On the East Coast of India its distribution is more extensive, being found and fished everywhere from Cape Comorin to Madras City. The northern limit on this coast may be placed at the mouths of the Godaveri, where I have found a few shells, all marked by stunted growth—individuals living in an unfavourable environment. The northern shores of Ceylon, from Puttalam in the north-west to Trincomalee on the north-east, yield large numbers of this shell; it is also to be found at the Andaman Islands.

The bottom most favoured of *Turbinella pyrum* is a sandy one containing a moderate proportion of mud; this character of bottom is admirably suited to the luxuriant growth of tube-building polychæt worms which constitute the main food supply of the chank. These polychæts are of several genera, the most abundant being Terebellids. In some places in the Gulf of Mannar, square miles of sea-bottom are monopolised by these Terebellids and the chanks and echinoderms which prey upon them; a veritable Terebella—Turbinella—Echinoderm formation. The edges of rocky reefs and the sandy patches interspersed among the rocks are other favourite haunts of chanks as the worms on which they prey are usually abundant there.

The shell of the adult chank is characteristically thick-walled and massive; in the live condition the exterior is covered with a dense brown and velvety horny layer, the periostracum; after death this dries, becomes brittle and eventually peels off, so that shells exposed for any length of time on the sea-shore or buried for any considerable period, become naked and reveal the characteristic snowy-white porcellaneous nature of the shell clearly. In fully grown shells the rows of chestnut brown spots which are normally very distinct on the outer surface in the immature, tend to disappear and often become entirely obliterated. Around the mouth, especially along the inner edge of the lip, a faint pink tint is often seen in fully mature shells, while occasionally the whole interior surface of the mouth may assume a brick-red colouration particularly in shells from certain localities. Characteristic of this genus are the three strong columellar plications or ridges upon the columella; the trace of a fourth is also frequently present.

Local races.—So considerable are the divergences in external form and colour shown by shells of normal individuals of *Turbinella pyrum* that conchologists have made several pseudo-species out of the principal variations. Intimate acquaintance, extending over a period of upwards of ten years, with all the chank-producing localities on the coasts of India and Ceylon, together with the advantage of having scrutinised several hundred thousand shells, convince me that all the so-called species of Turbinella found in Indian seas are referable to a single species—*T. pyrum*—and constitute, at the most, varieties of the nature of emphasized local races.

Three types exist which may be conveniently described as the obtuse, the central and the elongate. All three forms have their own particular geographical distribution and characteristic physical and biological environment. Normally they respectively occupy well-defined localities. Intermediate forms linking the different main varieties frequently occur, especially where the habitats of two varieties march, forming a debatable land where it becomes difficult or even impossible to assign the shells there found to one or other variety, so evenly are the respective characteristics balanced. But the vast bulk of the shells fall readily into one or other of the three types.

(*a*). The central variety preponderates largely over the other two; both numerically and industrially it is the most important and most valuable, being the form specially valued by the shell-bangle manufacturers of Bengal for the purposes of their trade. This type forms the bulk of the immense number fished off the Indian coast of the Gulf of Mannar and around the north of Ceylon, a number averaging some $1\frac{1}{2}$ million annually. Its range on the Indian coast is straitly limited on the north, where Pamban Pass and the north coast of Rameswaram Island at the head of the Gulf of Mannar mark the boundary, thence southward it extends along the shores of the Ramnad and Tinnevelly Districts. North-westward of Pamban Pass this variety marches with that which I shall term *obtusa*. Off Ceylon this central form is restricted to the northern coasts from the Pearl Banks and Mannar round to Trincomalee on the north-east coast.

Figs. 1 and 2.—Immature chanks from Okhamandal; both show persistence of the protoconch.

Fig. 3.—The Indian Chank, Turbinella pyrum, Linn., central type of form.

Fig. 4.—Elongated variety from the Andaman Islands. Adult and two very young specimens. The latter show the protoconch persisting.

[Figs. 1, 2, and 3 photographed by Vividha Kala Mandir, Baroda; Fig. 4 by Indian Museum, Calcutta.]

The central type has a heavy massive shell, with a well-proportioned and well-defined apical spiral. Apart from the chestnut coloured surface-markings which are extremely variable and tend to disappear with age, these shells are of an opalescent lily-white colour, porcellaneous in texture and slightly translucent when cut into sections. Unlike var. *obtusa* the colour of the body at the mouth is not deeply tinted ; usually it is of a very pale flesh tint or even quite white, whence comes the Tamil name *Vel-vayan* or " white-mouth " used to designate this variety, which again is split into several local races whereof the principal are known locally as (1) big-bellied chanks and (2) small-bellied chanks. The former come from the beds lying off the mouth of the Tambraparni River, the other chiefly from the northern beds off Tuticorin.

A second location of the central type is found on the coast of Kathiawar, separated from the Gulf of Mannar and Ceylon area by hundreds of miles of sea bottom from which all forms of *Turbinella pyrum* are absent.

(*b*). *Turbinella pyrum*, variety *obtusa*, is very distinctive in shape and sometimes in colouration. The apical spire is emphatically abbreviated, the whorls appearing as though telescoped while the colouring of the body at the mouth opening is frequently of a dark brick-red in shells from the Tanjore coast, most distinctive when compared with the delicate pallor of this region in shells of the central type.

The distribution of the *obtusa* variety includes the littoral waters of the eastern coast line of the Madras Presidency from Pamban Pass in Palk Bay to the delta of the Godaveri River in the north ; the chief fishing grounds are situated in Palk Bay and off the Tanjore coast, where this variety furnishes annually about 200,000 shells to the Calcutta market.

The shortening of the apical whorls often becomes extreme and so abbreviated as to be subtruncate and to approach in general form the aboral appearance of a typical *Conus*. This extreme form appears to arise when the environment is highly unfavourable, such as life in a muddy sea co-ordinated with scarcity of food ; it represents an extreme form of stunting, analogous to that seen on those pearl banks where dense over-population reduces the available food supply to a degree insufficient to meet the normal individual requirements.

(*c*). Variety *elongata* is a much elongated spindle-shaped form found in the Andaman Islands. As var. *obtusa* is the extreme in variation in the coniform direction so *elongata* approaches to the long-drawn-out spiral of *Fusus*. (Pl. II., fig. 4). Shells of this variety are very rare on the coast of the Indian mainland but I cannot accept it as anything more than a very well-marked variety of *Turbinella pyrum*.

The anatomy of the body of *Turbinella pyrum* follows closely the lines of such a typical gastropod as *Buccinum* (Whelk), and it is unnecessary to go into any details here, save to mention that the sexes are separate, the proboscis much elongated, and the columellar muscles extremely powerful. It is well nigh an impossibility to extract the animal intact from its shell even after death ; the ordinary methods which are readily successful in the case of *Buccinum* are ineffective here, and the aid of a sledge hammer has to be evoked if we require to dissect the animal.

The ova are deposited in a many-chambered chitinous egg-capsule of striking and peculiar appearance. In general form it is an elongated loosely spiral annulated cylinder, divided transversely by partitions into a number of compartments; it reminds one of a corrugated and loosely twisted ram's horn. When newly formed it is pale opaque yellow in colour; with age it darkens and becomes covered with low growths of algæ. It stands upright on the sea-bottom, the lower and first formed end rooted in the sand by means of a broad flange-shaped basal disc. The lower end is narrow, the chambers there small; these gradually increase in size, till at a point about one-third of the length from the base they attain a maximum size, which is maintained thence to the abruptly truncate summit.

Considerable complexity is introduced by the fact that the partitions between the chambers are double and separated by a slight space except along the hinder edge. The partition which forms the floor of each compartment has a crescentic slit parallel with the front edge, hence when the capsule sways to the current the partitions between the chambers gape slightly and so allow a circulation of sea-water within each compartment, thus providing the aeration needed by the larvæ. The transverse partitions are much thinner than the outer wall of the capsule.

In each chamber a considerable number of fertilised ova are deposited, embedded in a transparent colourless gelatinous nutritive matrix which entirely fills the chamber. In this nutritive jelly, the stronger of the embryos develop rapidly; in each chamber an average of six reach the larval stage characterised by the possession of a larval external shell or protoconch; those that do, grow rapidly and soon pass beyond the protoconch stage, and assume the semblance of adult form provided with a brown-flecked shell measuring eventually slightly over half an inch in length, inclusive of the two and a half whorls of the protoconch which persists both here and into adult life. By the time this size is attained all the nutritive contents of the incubatory chamber, including the remains of the weaker of the brethren, have been eaten up by the ravenous young who now find it necessary to leave home in search of food. Their first step is to eat through the partitions dividing the chambers, a proceeding that results in the bringing together of the whole surviving family numbering usually from 200 to 250 in all. The stronger next eat a way through the outer wall and the whole brood follow to scatter over the adjacent sea-bottom to lead independent lives.

The breeding season, when the capsules are fashioned and rooted in the sand, extends throughout January, February and the first half of March. Some divers assert that new capsules are also to be found in June and July, but I have had no opportunity to test this statement. The sexes being separate the divers have several stories to tell anent the breeding habits. Among others they assert that the females are the larger and are attended each by a number of smaller males, who assist in the making of the capsule—

a manifest impossibility. The post-larval rate of growth is quite unknown. On grounds where the food supply is abundant, it appears to be very rapid, for beds which are exhausted of adult shells measuring over $2\frac{1}{4}$ inches diameter in one year are found the succeeding year with plenty of shells, 3 inches and over in diameter.

The chank is an excellent instance of the acquisition by an animal of characters which appear for all practical purposes absolutely perfect to enable it to hold its own with ease in its struggle for existence. Against every one of its known enemies it has evolved suitable means of defence. The massive strength of the shell protects it from the attacks of all ordinary fishes ; the density and thickness of its periostracum give during youth and maturity adequate protection against the insidious attack of the boring sponge, *Cliona*, and its shell-burrowing congeners ; the strong capsule it constructs for its young gives them adequate protection till they reach a self-supporting stage endowed even at this early period with a fairly strong and resistant shell—one cannot crack it between one's finger and thumb. Its semi-burrowing habits give it great protection against those fishes which have the habit of snapping off the protruded feet of gastropods. Finally the pale yellowish-brown periostracum assimilates closely in colouring to the sand and should be a further protection against its discovery by foes ; to this form of protection I am, however, not inclined to assign great value, for chank divers can distinguish the presence of a chank even when half buried in the sand, and if they can, I feel assured that predatory fish are equally clever.

On rare occasions chank shells are found with the larger whorls crushed in ; this is believed to be the work of the great goggle-eyed Ray, *Rhinoptera adspersa,* which has the most powerful milling teeth of any Indian ray or shark.

As chanks grow old, their resisting powers diminish, the protecting periostracum receives damage and the burrowing sponge *Cliona* obtains a lodgment in the shell. Once there, it runs its branching tunnels everywhere in the substance of the shell, converting it into a honey-comb mass. I greatly doubt if this contributes except very occasionally to the death of the chank. This probably occurs usually from senile decay on beds that are not fished commercially. It is noteworthy that beds which have not been fished for some years, contain great numbers of Cliona-burrowed shells, whereas on beds fished regularly the proportion of " wormed " shells is so low as to be practically non-existent.

II

SOURCES OF INDUSTRIAL SUPPLY

EVERY year many lakhs of chank shells are required by the shell-bangle manufacturers of Dacca. To supply this demand hundreds of fishermen and divers, from Kathiawar in the north to Cape Comorin in the south, search the reefs and scour the sand-flats within the 10-fathom line during the fine weather season ; in some places they wade about in the shallows, in others they bring their catch to the surface in nets, or they may descend themselves to the bottom and hunt it by sight as they swim.

Six distinct chank fisheries are carried on at the present day in India seas ; ranked in their geographical order they are situated in the following localities :—

(*a*). Kathiawar ;
(*b*). Travancore ;
(*c*). The Gulf of Mannar (usually called the Tuticorin Fishery) ;
(*d*). Palk Strait (known generally as the Rameswaram and Ceylon Fisheries) ;
(*e*). The Coromandel Coast, from Point Calimere to Madras City.

Without exception the chank fishery in each of these localities is considered as a royal prerogative, the monopoly of Government. In practice this prerogative is variously exercised. In the Gulf of Mannar and on the Indian side of Palk Strait, the Madras Government work the fishery departmentally through an officer of the Fisheries Department styled the Superintendent of Pearl and Chank Fisheries. On the Coromandel coast the exclusive right to collect is farmed out to a renter for a term of years. The latter administration of the prerogative is also in force in Okhamandal (Kathiawar), where His Highness the Gaekwar of Baroda exercises sovereign rights in the local fishery. In Ceylon the renting system was in force till 1890, when it was abandoned in favour of an export duty, a method of securing Government revenue from this source which has continued ever since. In Travancore the dues of Government are collected in the same manner as now prevails in Ceylon.

The shells fished off the Kathiawar coast are of good quality, well esteemed in the Bengal trade where they are known as Sūrti shells—an echo of the day when Surat was the great emporium of the Kathiawar and Konkan coasts. To-day the shells are sent to Bombay, whence they are shipped to Calcutta. The quantity yielded is approximately 200 to 250 bags per annum.

Okhamandal, the north-western extremity of Kathiawar, which forms an outlying portion of the Gaekwar of Baroda's dominions, furnishes a considerable proportion of this export. The right to collect the shells is leased out at intervals for a term of years. Unlike other Indian chank fisheries the shells on this coast are all collected at spring tides when great areas of the littoral are uncovered at the time of low water. A certain proportion of the shells are sold to pilgrims who resort to the holy shrines at Bēt and Dwarka, the district of Okhamandal from its association with Krishna forming one of the holy lands of the Hindus, who delight to take home as a sacred souvenir one of the shells loved of this god. Full details of this fishery and of the enactments made to safeguard it, are to be found in Part I of the present Report.

Were diving for these shells to be introduced on the Kathiawar coast a great increase in the yield should be possible. As it is, the warm weather when alone diving can be systematically carried on is unfortunately that when the monsoon is most violent.

The chief centres of supply at the present day are the Gulf of Mannar and Palk Bay where physical and climatic conditions permit of diving being ultilised to an extent impossible in any of the other fisheries. Indeed chank-diving in these waters has been the regular calling of hundreds of the fishing population from time immemorial and references in Tamil classics make it clear that this fishery was prosecuted with vigour under Pandyan rule as long ago as the beginning of the Christian era ; in those days the headquarters of the industry was at Korkai, an important emporium with a population composed, we are told, in the main of traders, jewellers, pearl-fishers and chank divers. This city, the Kolkhoi of Greek geographers, was situated at the mouth of the Tambraparni which then entered the sea some 12 miles south of the present-day port of Tuticorin.

The relative importance of the various centres is shown clearly in the following table compiled from the Bengal customs returns for the eight years from 1905-1913.

TABLE SHOWING THE VALUE OF IMPORTS OF CHANK SHELLS INTO CALCUTTA FROM 1905 to 1913.

	1905–1906.	1906–1907.	1907–1908.	1908–1909.	1909–1910.	1910–1911.	1911–1912.	1912–1913.
	Rs.	Rs.	Rs.	Rs.	Rs.	Rs.	Rs.	Rs.
From Ceylon ...	144,772	189,280	86,515	181,223	166,060	87,716	133,495	127,940
From Madras—								
Chief Port ...	1,583	14,435	324	2,842	1,648	1,945	2,025	3,086
Other Ports ...	32,172	21,622	5,265	52,399	66,371	44,504	65,600	74,153
Travancore	114	—	592	—	500	—	96	—
Bombay*	?	?	?	?	?	?	?	?
Total ... Rs.	178,641	225,337	92,696	236,464	234,579	134,165	201,216	205,179

* Not ascertainable as chanks and cowries have been lumped together in the Customs returns of the Bombay exports.

The export from Bombay consists solely of shells fished on the Kathiawar coast, so far as I am able to learn. These "Sūrti" shells, as they are known in trade circles, share with the Tuticorin and Rameswaram shells the honour of being esteemed of first quality. To-day these shells command an average price of not less than Rs. 180 per 1,000 in the wholesale market at Calcutta.

From the foregoing facts it is abundantly clear that, barring the pearl fisheries of the Gulf of Mannar, the chank fishery is beyond comparison the most important of Indian shell-fish industries. Year in and year out the chank fishery produces regularly from 2 to 2½ lakhs of rupees per annum (£13,300 to £16,600) whereas the pearl fishery may prove wholly unproductive for many years together, though when it does yield a return, it does so with no niggard hand. The pearl fishery owes much to the chank-fishery; the latter is the school where boys and men of the fisher population pass their apprenticeship and qualify for the feverish days of a pearl fishery—a time when a gambler's lust for gain enters the diver's breast and makes him forget or ignore danger, and despise sleep and comfort in the race to gather the pearly treasures put at his disposal for an all-too-brief season, counted by days, and limited by the tempest.

III

THE ROLE PLAYED BY THE CHANK IN INDIAN RELIGION AND LIFE

(1). Legendary and Historical.

When and how the cult of the chank as a religious symbol originated in India are questions going back so far beyond any traditions now existing that the utmost difficulty confronts us when we seek to find their solution. One main fact alone seems certain and that is the non-Aryan origin of this symbol. The Aryan-speaking hordes which descended upon the Punjab through the N.W. passes perhaps 2,000 years or more B.C., certainly did not bring the custom with them. They, the warrior ploughmen and herdsmen of the plains of Eastern Europe and Western Asia, had never seen the sea; they knew not as yet the deep sonorous boom of the snow-white chank—a note on a curved cattle-horn was with them the signal between scattered bands, while their hymns tell us that in music they used the drum, the flute and the lute. Vishnu, the God whose emblems include the chank, is barely mentioned in the Rig-Veda and the few Vedic hymns to him were probably composed after long intercourse had been established with the Dravidians, the chief race whom the invaders found in possession of the new land. He is almost certainly one of the gods borrowed from the indigenous people as his complexion is characteristically represented as dark-hued whenever his image is shown in colour.

I am strongly of opinion that the key to the problem is to be sought in the custom prevalent among animists—the worshippers of evil spirits—of employing noise to scare the demons they fear. At the present day Bengali Hindus make a practice of sounding the conch which each household keeps for religious rites whenever an eclipse or an earthquake occurs. Clearly this is a survival of the use of loud blasts on a shell to scare away evil spirits—the demon intent on devouring the moon or the sun, or shaking in fury the foundations of the world. This custom at once conferred religious significance upon the shell whose noise frightens the evil spirit and restores peace; thenceforward the shell would be honoured and held sacred. Probably it was associated with one particular god, the prototype of Vishnu, and, with his adoption into the Aryan Pantheon, his emblem and weapon against the powers of evil would accompany him, and become endowed with still greater and deeper religious significance.

When the hungry swarms of Aryan tribesmen descended upon north-west India, the whole land, with the exception of the north-east corner, was occupied by a long-settled aboriginal population, split into many states and tribes vastly differing in civilisation. Many tribes, particularly those living in the mountains and dense forests and less accessible districts, were in the lowest possible stage, naked savages living on fruits and small game and maintaining a precarious defence against wild beasts by means of rude stone weapons and cudgels. In the south, especially in the maritime districts, a high civilisation developed at a comparatively early date and when the Aryan invaders were fighting their way into the Punjab against wild and semi-savage tribes, in appearance and customs probably much like the Santals 50 years ago, the men of the south were then or shortly later engaged in commercial relations with Babylon and the coastal districts of the Persian Gulf and Red Sea; partly through the stimulation received from this intercourse with these seats of ancient civilisation and partly from indigenous effort these southern Dravidians were evolving a language unsurpassed for its richness and flexibility and its power to express with perfect felicity the highest flights of imagination which poets and philosophers can reach, together with a material civilisation of no mean order. It is to these coastal Dravidians settled in the prosperous sea-ports situated on the western shore of the Gulf of Mannar or to men of the same race living on the Kathiawar coast that the first use of the chank must be traced. Both localities were the seats of pearl fisheries and the centres whence much oversea traffic flowed coastwise to Persia, Egypt and the adjacent Semitic lands. The chank and the pearl-oyster are usually associated in Indian waters, the chank on the sandy patches interspersed with the rocky patches which form the habitat of the pearl-oyster; pearl fishers often bring chanks ashore and thus the beauty of their snowy white porcelain-like massive shells would early become familiar to the merchants gathered from many lands to purchase pearls.

The word itself, in its chief forms of *chanku* or *sanku* in Tamil and *sankha* in Sanscrit, appears to be of Aryan origin; the Indian names are all obviously variants of one root and this is identifiable with the Greek *kongche* (κόγχη) and the Latin *concha*, both meaning a shell. It is probable that when the Aryans swarmed into India they applied their generic name for shells to the great white conch so conspicuous an object in the hands of their enemies, and so it is that, just as Christians in calling their scriptures by the Greek word for book (Biblos) imply thereby that it is "The Book" pre-eminent and supreme, so the Aryans appear to have similarly lauded the chank as "The Shell" and considered no qualifying term necessary. To them it was the shell of shells—the one shell above all others worthy of honour and even of worship. In the oldest Tamil literature the word is found in its present-day form but almost as often the shell is termed *vălai*; the latter is probably the original Tamil or Dravidian name, a term which has now come to be displaced by one derived from the Sanscrit *sankha*.

We may infer that when these ancient poems were written the Brahmans had already acquired great influence and were engaged in forcing Aryan forms and Sanscrit terms into the language of the Tamil country by virtue of their religious and literary ascendancy. As the religious leaders of the country, Sanscrit terms in constant use in their prayers and services would soon become dominant and be absorbed into the language of the country, in the way that Norman culinary terms readily found acceptance in the English language because of the superiority of the Normans to the Saxons in this particular art. Thus it has happened that the Sanscrit term for *Turbinella pyrum* gradually but surely ousted the indigenous Tamil term. Finally it is worthy of note that the English word " conch " is again another variant of the words chanku and sankha.

The earliest notices of the use of the chank are entirely of a secular nature, and occur in the two great Indian epics, the Ramayana and the Mahabharata. In these we get frequent reference to the employment of the chank as a martial trumpet by the great warriors whose more or less mythical exploits are recounted. Particularly is this the case in the Mahabharata, where in the Bhagavat-Gita we find the heroes endeavouring to terrify their foes with loud blasts on their battle-conchs, even as their forefathers scared away the evil-working spirits of the village. Each hero has his famous conch distinguished by some high-sounding name, just as the famous swords of European legendary heroes were frequently given names that have become immortal in song and story. The beautiful Excalibur wielded by Arthur in many glorious fights, Charlemagne's famous Joyeuse, and the magic Tyrfing so oft the theme of Viking sagas, have their parallels in the names of the conchs of the Mahabharata heroes.

When the opposing hosts of Kauravas and Pandavas confronted each other on the field of Kurukshetra, we read in the Bhagavat-Gita (verses 11 to 19) how the prelude to battle was the deafening clamour sounded by the leaders on their great conchs.

" The Ancient of the Kurus, the Grandsire (Bhisma), the glorious, sounded on high his conch, ' The Lion's Roar.'

" Then conchs and kettledrums, tabors and drums and cowhorns suddenly blared forth with tumultuous clamour.

" Stationed in their great war-chariot yoked to white horses, Mādhava (Krishna) and the son of Pāndu (Arjuna) blew their divine conchs.

" Panchajanya was blown by Hrishikisha (Krishna) and Devadatta by Dhananjaya (Arjuna). Vrikodara (Bhima) of terrible deeds blew his mighty conch, Paundra.

" The king Yudhishthira, the son of Kunti, blew Anantavijaya ; Nakula and Sahadeva blew their conchs Sughosha and Manipushpaka.

" And Kāshya of the great bow, and Shikhandi, the mighty carwarrior, Dristadyumna and Virata and Sātykai, the unconquered.

" Drupada and the Draupadeyas, O Lord of Earth, and Saubhadra, the mighty-armed, on all sides their several conchs blew.

" That tumultuous uproar rent the hearts of the sons of Dhritarashtra, filling the earth and sky with sound."

Here the names of the conchs possessed by all the five Pandava brothers are given,

—Paundra, Devadatta, Anantavijaya, Sughosha and Manipushpaka. Paundra appears to have been named from Pundra, a demon killed by Bhima; the others signify respectively God-given, Eternal Victory, Sweet Voice or Honey-tone, and Jewel-blossom.

Here too we hear for the first time the name Panchajanya given to the conch of Krishna, King of the Yādavas, who had espoused the Pandavan cause. Around this famous shell many legends have gathered and now we see it held on high in most figures of Vishnu, who is considered by Hindus to have been re-incarnated in Krishna, the wise and good king of the Yādavas. According to one legend Panchajanya was originally the shell home of a terrible marine demon, Panchajana, so named as he was a foe to the five kinds of beings (*jana*), to wit, gods, men, gandharvas, serpents and ghosts or non-incorporated spirits. Panchajana lived on the sea bottom and at last filled the measure of his misdeeds by seizing the son of Sandipani, who had taught Krishna the use of arms. The God, fearless of consequences, rushed to the help of the child, assuming the form of a fish; after a terrible struggle he vanquished the demon and brought away his shell as a trophy, since accounted one of the emblems of Vishnu and Krishna.

Tod, the author of the famous *Annals of Rajasthan*, in his "Travels in Western India," published 1839, in describing his visit to Dwarka and its neighbourhood gives a variant of this story and as the passage is most interesting no apology is needed for its reproduction in full. Under date January 1, 1823, he writes, "Crossed over to the Pirates' isle, emphatically called Bate, or 'the island,' but in the classic traditions of the Hindu, Sankhodwara, or 'the door of the shell,' one of the most sacred spots of his faith. It was here that Crishna [1] or Kanya acted the part of the Pythian Apollo, and redeemed the sacred books, slaying his hydra foe, Takshac, who had purloined and concealed them in one of those gigantic shells whence the island has its name. The whole history of Kanya, or Crishna, who assumed the form of Vishnu, is allegorical, but neither devoid of interest nor incapable of solution. There is no part of their mythology more easy of illustration than this, which is allusive to the sectarian warfare carried on at this period between the new sect of Vishnuvites and the more ancient one of Budha. The races who supported the religion of Crishna are typified under his emblem, Garuda, or the eagle; while their wily adversary, the Budhist, is figured by the Tacshac, Naga, or serpent, a denomination given to the races of northern origin, which at various periods overran India, and of which were Taksiles (the friend of Alexander, the site of whose capital is still preserved in the Memoirs of Baber) and the still more famed Tacshac Salivahan, the foe of Vikrama. In the legend of the Yadu (Yadava) prince, Crishna (himself a seceder from the faith of Budha Trivicrama to that of Vishnu, if not its founder), receiving the sacred volumes from his hydra foe at this

[1] Tod notes "Kanya, or Vishnu, resembles the sun-god of the Egyptians in name as well as symbols. Kan was one name of the sun in Egypt, and his eagle-head is a well-known type." With regard to the extract given in the text, it has to be remembered that Tod's mythological explanations are not always reliable.

remote point of Hinduism, as well as his first combat with him in the Jumna, we have but the continuance of the same sectarian warfare, in which Crishna was in this instance successful, driving them before him both in the north of India and here: thus, his title of *Rinchor* was given on his defeat by Jarasindha, the King of Magadha, of the heretical faith, and at length these religious and civil conflicts led to his death, and the dispersion of the Yadu race of which he was the chief support. These Yadus, I surmise to have been all originally Budhists, and of Indo-Getic origin, as their habits of polyandrism alone would almost demonstrate; and when we find the best-informed of the Jains assuring us that Nemnat'h, the twenty-second Budha, was not only Yadu, but the near kinsman of Crishna, all doubt is at an end; and I am strongly inclined to pronounce decidedly, what I have before only suggested, that the Yadus are the Yute, or ancient Getes of the Jaxartes, amongst whom, according to Professor Newmann from Chinese authorities, one of the Shamanean sages sprung, eight hundred years before Christ. Both Nemnat'h and Sham-nat'h have the same personal epithets, derived from their dark complexions, the first being familiarly called Arishta-Nemi, 'the black Nemi,' the other Sham and Crishna, both also meaning 'dark-coloured'; and when this is not only confirmed by tradition, but the shrine of Budha itself is yet preserved within that of Crishna at Dwarica we have no reason to question that his faith, prior to his own deification, was that of Budha."

Always is Krishna's chank represented as a sinistral abnormality, and legend pictures to the mind of the devout Hindu every shell of this rare form when alive as a marvellous production receiving the homage of thousands of chanks of ordinary form, which crowd around it on all sides. Another myth is related by Baldæus, the chaplain to the Dutch forces which wrested Ceylon from the Portuguese, to the effect that Garuda, the eagle vehicle or attendant (almost certainly the hawk-headed deity of Assyria) of Vishnu flew in all haste to Brahma and brought to Krishna "the chianko or kink-horn twisted to the right."[1] Vishnu derives several of his alternative names from his chank symbol, as Chankapāni, the "chank-armed," and Chankamēnthi, the "chank-bearer."

Krishna, when represented as a herdsman under the form of Govinda or Gopala, usually bears a conch in his hand and possibly the origin of this may be sought in the use a herdsman may make of it to call together his scattered charge just as the shepherds of Corsica and Sardinia at the present day use a great Triton shell (*Tritonium noduliferum*) for a like purpose.

A curious and most significant fact is that the twenty-second Tirthankar of the Jains, Nemi or Nemnath, who, legend says, was the son of King Samudravijaya of the race

[1] With the contradiction which exists between East and West in so many matters, the abnormal twist in these shells is termed the left-handed or sinistral by Europeans, whereas Indians term it right-handed. They view it from the mouth end, we from the apex, and accordingly confusion is frequent in conversation on this subject with Indians.

of Harivansa and a cousin to Krishna, has a conch as his emblem and is represented in Jain statues as being of a black colour. The black image of Nemi in the Nemnath temple on Mount Girnar in Kathiawar is a well-known example. The dark hue under which Vishnu and Krishna are always represented by Hindus and the black colour of his cousin Nemi, the Jain Tirthankar, go far to show that these gods and teachers belonged not to the Aryan race but to nations of Dravidian origin in the forefront of the earliest indigenous civilization in North India or Hindustan. With them in particular, is the conch most definitely associated; there is strong presumption on this and other grounds already referred to, to believe that it was the Dravidians who first employed the chank as a battle-conch and that this custom was adopted by the Aryan invaders as blood connections began to be formed in increasing numbers with the Dravidian nobility of the land and when certain of the Dravidian gods were admitted to the Aryan pantheon. The Aryans would be particularly eager to acquire fine conchs both for use and ornament; their deep-voiced boom would prove their utility as battle-trumpets to enspirit and to give signals, while their rare white beauty would appeal to the religious sense as making them fit vessels wherewith to offer libations to their gods. To an inland people the beautiful products of the sea assume a double value from their strangeness and rarity and mysterious origin. To-day the people of Tibet, cut off from all knowledge of the sea, esteem pearls and red coral, tortoise-shell and amber, among the greatest treasures within their knowledge. The wild Nagas of the Assam hills equally prized the snow-white chank shell itself till some 50 years ago, using it as part of their accepted currency at the rates enumerated on page 43. As the Aryan hosts advanced into India they must have captured numbers of battle conchs from time to time and there can be no doubt they early adopted them in place of their own less sonorous cow-horns. Indeed the boom of the conch has been the battle signal throughout the ages in India, and this custom has lasted almost to the present day. Ancient Tamil and Rajput poems descriptive of battles and raids continually refer to the clamour of the conchs blown as the opposing parties approached each other; the etiquette of old Indian chivalry required a prelude of challenging conch-blowing before the serious fight was begun; the long-drawn hollow sonorous note of the chank often greeted early British commanders as they led their forces to the assault; until the beginning of last century Marathi and Pindari chiefs called their followers together and heartened them for the fray by loud blasts on conch-horns. Even in very recent days the chank's voice has called our enemies to the attack, and this too by other foes than Hindus. The graphic pen of Percival Landon in his "Lhasa"—an account of the British Mission to Thibet in 1903-4, in describing a night cannonade of the British Commissioner's post outside of Gyantse by the Thibetans, paints a word picture worthy of quotation:—"As one peers out into the warm night a long monotone is faintly droned out from the darkness ahead. It is one of the huge conch shells in the jong and it may only mean a call to prayer—the 'hours' of Lamaism are unending—but as the moaning note persists softly and steadily a vivid speck of flame stabs the darkness across the river. A second later the report of the gun accompanies a prolonged 'the-e-es' overhead."

From the earliest times the conch has also been used in India to call the people to their sacrifices and other religious rites, as an instrument of invocation to call the attention of the gods to the ceremonies to be performed, and as a means to keep evil spirits at a distance and to prevent their entry into houses and temples.

With this intimate association with the chief religious rites, the people gradually came to reverence the instrument itself, and to adore and invoke it (see p. 22 for details), as is also done with regard to many other instruments or articles of sacrifice in Hindu rites at the present day; these latter do not, however, appeal in equal measure to the religious feelings of the multitude, for around them have not been woven the myths and legends pertaining to the chank.

In the ceremonies attending the coronation of great kings the chank naturally played an important part. At the time when the Mahabharata was put into its present form, this custom was fully developed to judge from the description of the coronation of King Yudhistira given in the Shantiparwa of that epic. To quote from an interesting summary by Rao Sahib P. B. Joshi[1] "Kings of different countries, learned Brahmans and sages were invited for the ceremony. A *Vedi* or sacrificial altar was prepared. There were brought *Samidhas* or pieces of sacred wood, five kinds of sacred leaves, waters of the holy rivers and of the four seas, seven kinds of holy earth, the sacred conch shell, a white umbrella, and white *Chamars*. The horses and elephants used in connection with the coronation ceremony were also white. Yudhistir was then made to sit on a throne of gold, and other members of the royal family sat on seats made of ivory, and close by sat the king's spiritual guide and other sages. The king was now requested to touch such auspicious articles as corn, white flowers, swastika, gold, silver and jewels. The king's ministers and other high functionaries were now brought before him by the royal priest and they all paid their homage to their sovereign. The sacred fire was then kindled, the king and queen sat in front of the holy fire on seats covered over with tiger's skin, and made offerings to the fire. Shri Krishna then got up, took in his hand the sacred conch-shell, which was filled with holy water, sprinkled the water over the heads of the king and queen and said: 'I sprinkle this holy water over you to indicate that from this day you have become the paramount sovereign of Bharat Varsha.' At this time *dhundubi* and other musical instruments were sounded, drums were beaten, the king's bards sang the praise of the king and wished him victory and long life."

In Bengal every marriage conducted according to Hindu ceremonial includes the placing of chank-bangles, lacquered red, upon the bride's wrists. An iron bangle placed on the left wrist is also essential to the ceremony. Elsewhere this particular marriage custom is scarcely ever practised, but sufficient instances are recorded among a few widely scattered castes and caste-sections of the existence of a similar marriage custom

[1] *The Times of India Illustrated Weekly*, 20th September, 1911.

elsewhere to tempt us to believe that at one time it was the general custom of all fully Hinduised castes throughout India. Finds of fragments of chank-bangles in places where the use of these ornaments is non-existent at the present day strengthen the theory. Legendary lore can also be quoted in support. For instance, among the Balijas of Telugu districts, who there constitute the chief trading caste, a legend is current (Thurston, I, p. 137) that " on one occasion Siva wanted his consort Parvati to appear before him in all her glory. But, when she stood before him, fully decorated, he laughed and said that she was not as charming as she might be. On this, she prayed that Siva would help her to become so. From his braid of hair Siva created a being who descended on the earth, bearing a number of bangles and turmeric paste, with which Parvati adorned herself. Siva, being greatly pleased with her appearance, told her to look at herself in a looking-glass. The being who brought the bangles is believed to have been the ancestor of the Gāzula Balijas."

The latter sub-division of the Balijas peddle glass bangles only at the present day, but it is reasonable to suppose that before the discovery of glass, their stock in trade consisted instead of chank bangles. It is indeed probable that the introduction of glass dealt a heavy blow to the employment of the chank shell in feminine adornment in certain districts, particularly, for instance, in those where, as in Vizagapatam, glass factories being established, glass bangles were put on sale at a fraction of the cost of the comparatively expensive chank ones, which require the expenditure of much time and labour to render them attractive.

Another legend, prevalent among the Sangukatti Idaiyans, the great pastoral or shepherd caste of Tamil India, narrates that when Krishna desired to marry Rukmani, her family insisted on marrying her to Sishupalen. When the wedding was about to take place, Krishna carried off Rukmani and placed a bangle made of chank-shell on her wrist (Thurston, II, p. 354). These particular Idaiyans belong to one of the sections of this caste which to-day require their married women to wear these bangles—now a very rare custom in South India.

Indian sources give the barest indications of the traffic in chank shells that must have been brisk for 3,000 years or more between the fisheries in the Gulf of Mannar and on the Kathiawar coast and the inland nations of the Deccan and Hindustan.

(2) Present Day Uses.

(a) In religious ceremonial (including marriage and death rites), and vulgar superstition.

We have already seen that the chank is one of the two most important symbols—the other being the wheel or chakram—associated by Hindus with Vishnu, the second person in the Brahmanic trinity or Trimurthi. The majority of the avatars or incarnations of Vishnu are also occasionally represented as holding a chank in the hand: Matsya, in the form of a fish, Kurma the tortoise, Varaha the boar, and Narsingha the man-lion, are avatars sometimes sculptured holding Vishnu's chank: more frequently Krishna is thus depicted. Narayana, the god dwelling in the sun, another form of Vishnu, is similarly represented in human form with a chank in one hand and a discus (chakram) in the other. On rare occasions Siva is also depicted as holding a chank in one hand. In all these instances the chank represented is of the sinistral or left-handed form, a rarity so choice and valuable as to be worthy to form an adornment of a god. No more fitting gift to a deity can be imagined; as the symbol of the god who divides with Siva the worship of the Hindu world, as a production of nature so scarce as to appear once only in several millions of normally shaped shells and as an emblem of purity, could Hindu find more fitting offering at the shrine of his god? Thus it is that the pious wealthy have from time to time dedicated these shells to favourite temples—particularly to those that are in high esteem at centres of Hindu pilgrimage.

Chanks are held in special veneration at those shrines where the cult of Krishna is the predominant feature of worship, and in those localities rendered sacred to Hindus because of their reputed association with this deity while sojourning on earth.

Chief among the former is the great religious centre of the Madhva sect at Udipi in South Canara. There around a temple dedicated to Krishna are disposed eight mutts, or religious colleges, whereof the priesthood is a peregrinating fraternity, who tour the country to confirm in their faith the scattered members of their community— a procedure which consists in branding with hot irons the deity's symbols of the chank and the wheel upon the arms of the faithful.

Usually the priests of seven mutts are on tour; the head of one mutt takes charge in rotation of the Udipi temple and for a period of two years carries on the services and provides the funds necessary for the lavish charity dispensed daily by the temple.

The members of this sect have a great reputation for active piety and the priesthood of each mutt vie with those of the others in collecting precious vessels for use in the service of the deity. The sinistral chank is the principal of these, and so it comes about that in the eight mutts at Udipi is gathered an unique collection of these rarities. During a recent visit to this place the Swamiyar or high-priest was good enough to show me the four which belong to his mutt—the Puttigé mutt. Of these, two were handsomely mounted in richly chased gold, the others in silver. All were rather small in size and one appeared to be of the sub-fossil description frequently found buried in muddy deposits in shallow lagoons in the north of Ceylon. A census of the sinistral shells possessed by the whole eight mutts was not possible, but from the information received from the high priest there cannot be less than thirty of these shells in the town, allowing the low average of three to each mutt and six for those possessed by wealthy Hindus who are not of the priesthood.

After Udipi, probably the largest number of sinistral chanks are to be found in the temples of the sacred land of Kathiawar, rich in its association with the later life of Krishna ; while in Bet in 1906, I found richly ornamented sinistral chanks in the Shank Narayan, Lakhsmi and Satya Bhamaji temples. (Plate I.) That in the last named is a particularly large and handsome shell, probably the finest sinistral chank in existence and consequently an almost priceless treasure. The shell possessed by the Shank Narayan temple is a small elongated specimen offered at the shrine some twenty years ago by a Bathia from Zanzibar ; that of the Laksmi temple is a short broad one of small size with handsome arabesque ornamentation on the mounting—it has been in the possession of the temple since Samvat 1890 (A.D. 1835). At Benares, temple treasures include similar examples, while in the south of India, where opportunities to obtain these shells are great, a considerable number of the temples of that devout land possess one or more. Those at Rameswaram, Trichendur and Madura may be instanced.

The temple at Rameswaram, one of the four most holy places of pilgrimage among Hindus, possesses four shells ; of these three are very ancient and date from the days when the munificence of the Madura and Ramnad rulers endowed this temple with a share of the produce of the local pearl and chank fisheries. The shells in the Trichendur Temple, a towering pile overlooking a sea where chank fishing still flourishes, are derived likewise from a privilege share possessed formerly by the temple in this fishery.

It is noteworthy that although Rama, an incarnation of Vishnu, is especially associated with the Rameswaram temple, the actual deity represented in the inmost shrine is the phallic lingam of Siva. On important religious festivals water is poured into the sinistral chanks, and after Vedic chants have been sung and prayers offered, the water thus consecrated is poured over the lingam.

It is remarkable also and indicative that this custom has not originated with modern Hinduism, that sinistral chanks are objects of adoration among northern Buddhists. Sarat Chandra Das, the intrepid survey officer who spent some perilous years in Thibet, mentions (*Journey to Lhasa*, London, 1902) that in the Sakya Monastery lying to the south-west of Shigatze there is preserved in the temple a chank of this rare form. Its history is invested with more than ordinary interest, for the monastic records state that it was a present from Kublai Khan, the great Tartar conqueror of China and patron of the Polos, to Phagpa, a hierarch of Sakya whom Kublai made ruler of Thibet in the second half of the thirteenth century. Sarat Chandra Das mentions that this famous shell is blown by the lamas only when the request is accompanied by a present of seven ounces of silver, but to have it blown " is held to be an act of great merit."

In Thibet these left-handed chanks are called *Ya chvil dung-kar* and in Chinese *Yu hsuan pai-lei*. The people of both countries consider such shells as treasures of inestimable value. In 1867, one was known to be kept at Fuchu by the Ti-tuh (*Peking Gazette*, February 23rd, 1867) and one at Lhasa (*fide* an editorial note in Das, " *Journey to Lhasa*," above quoted).

At one time the value of these shells is said to have been assessed at their weight in gold and this statement is probably correct. To-day they are less valuable and small and imperfect ones occasionally change hands in the north of Ceylon at Rs. 60 to Rs. 90 each (say £4 to £6); such shells are usually sub-fossil ones found buried in deep mud. Large good-conditioned sinistral shells obtained alive, and therefore of good colour, still command high rates—anything from Rs. 400 to Rs. 5,000 or more—so infrequently are they found.

The method of estimating the approximate value of these latter shells is as follows—if the shell be of 100 rupees' weight or over (one standard coin weighs exactly one tola; 2½ tolas = one ounce) the value is calculated at the rate of Rs. 50 per tola or rupee's weight; thus a shell of 110 rupees' weight would be estimated accordingly to this method at Rs. 5,500. When the weight is between 30 and 100 tolas then the rate per tola may be taken at Rs. 30/- to Rs. 40/- according to size and quality; a 50 tola weight shell would be worth from Rs. 1,500 to Rs. 2,000. If of 25 tolas' weight the rate may vary from Rs. 5/- to Rs. 20/- per tola.

Wealthy Hindu Rajahs and Zamindars also aspire to possess these sacrosanct shells, the orthodox in order that they may use them to perform *abeyshekam* [1] in their family shrine and others for the ostentatious pride of possession and because of the superstition generally current which accounts the ownership of a Valampuri chank as conferring prosperity upon the household owning it.

I know also a wealthy Muhammadan Marakkayar who has refused offers of several hundreds of rupees for one of these shells; to him the shell is a mascot, the bringer of good luck.

The result of my inquiries indicates that there exist at present in India not less than 120 sinistral chank shells. I know the actual whereabouts of 60 and I am well satisfied that it is improbable that I have overestimated the remainder at an equal number.

The chank shell is so massive and strong as to be practically indestructible under ordinary circumstances. I have found chank artifacts in the ruins of Korkai, the Kolkhoi of the old Greek and Egyptian geographers, which though over 1,000 years old are indistinguishable except in colour from fragments cut in Dacca workshops to-day. Hence the sinistral shells now found in Hindu temples should represent the aggregate catch of this abnormality for several hundreds of years. If we place the period at the conservative limit of 300 years we shall find the percentage borne by sinistral to normal dextral shells an extremely small one. Elsewhere (Madras Fisheries Bulletin, No. 7) I have shown that the average catch of chank shells off the Indian and Ceylon coasts aggregates 2,500,000 per annum. There is reason to believe that a hundred years ago the average was considerably higher but some allowance must be made for interruptions in the fishery due to political unrest in the troublous times prior to the coming of the *Pax Britannica*. 2½ millions of shells are therefore probably a fairly accurate approxi-

[1] The worship of the gods with libations.

mation. At this rate the produce of the past 300 years would amount to a total of 750,000,000 shells; the 120 sinistral shells believed to exist now thus give the infinitesimal ratio of one shell to 6¼ millions of normal ones, and this proportion undoubtedly gives a substantially accurate idea of the great rarity of the abnormal form.

Among the ignorant who usually have never even seen a Valampuri chank, the belief is prevalent in Tamil South India that it blows of its own accord during the night; even the Roman Catholic chank divers of Tuticorin entertain this quaint superstition, and say that the shell is specially clamorous on Tuesday and Friday nights! A yogi when controlling or retaining his breath is also credited with hearing the sound of a Valampuri chank blowing within his abdomen though why the rumbling should be that of a Valampuri and not of an ordinary chank is hard to answer.

Worship of the chank as one of the three essential articles used in domestic worship among Brahmans should occupy an important part in the daily liturgy of this priestly caste and in the Brahma Karma, the work which sets forth in minute detail the order and phrasing of the sacred rites of the Brahmans, the prayer to the sacred chank may be translated as follows:—

Taking the chank in his hand the Brahman recites: "At the mouth of this shell is the God of the Moon, on its sides is Varuna, on its back Prajāpati, and on its apex the Ganges, the Sarasvati, and all the other sacred rivers of the three worlds in which they make ablutions according to the command of Vāsudeva.[1] In this chank is the chief of the Brahmans (Brahmendra or Brahmanaspati). This is why we must worship the sacred chank. Glory to thee, sacred shell, blessed by all the gods, born in the sea, and formerly held by Vishnu in his hand. We adore the sacred chank and meditate upon it. May we be filled with joy!

"I offer (to the chank) everything needful for worship—perfumes, rice and flowers."

Here they make the sign of the chank, but Bourquin ("Annales du Musée Guimet," Vol. VII, p. 45), from whom I quote, says he was never able to discover the manner of making this sign and I have had a like ill-success.

While the above is a portion of the liturgy which the head of each Brahman family is theoretically bound to recite daily, under present-day conditions this is impossible, and in fact it is only on specially important puja or holy days that even a greatly curtailed version of this and the accompanying prayers is recited by the head of the family, and this, too, only in thoroughly orthodox families. The curtailed prayer usually runs, "Oh, chank shell, thou wast produced in the sea and art held by Vishnu in his hand. Thou art worshipped by all the gods. Receive my homage."

In this connection an interesting chank legend centres round the temple tank in Tirukalikundram, a holy Saivite village in the Chingleput District, some 37 miles southward of Madras. The village munsiff, Mr. T. A. Vedachala Gurukkal, to whom I am indebted for the following particulars, states that once every twelve years a chank rises

[1] One of the names of Krishna.

to the surface of the large sacred bathing tank called Sanku Theertham. Three days before this marvellous occurrence, the water in the tank is greatly agitated, foaming and boiling to the accompaniment of considerable noise. On the appearance of the chank the foam subsides and the sound ceases. Then the chank comes to the side where it is picked up, purified and holy water sprinkled upon it. Thus consecrated it is carried in solemn procession through the village to the Vethagiriswarar temple, where it is placed in the treasury with the rest of the temple treasures.

Locally this chank is considered superior to all other chanks in the world and the origin of the periodic miracle is narrated as follows :—

When the sage Mārkkandēya was visiting the sacred places with his disciple, the latter forgot to bring the Siva puja-box containing the chank required for the libation necessary in the ritual of worship. The sage took his bath in the tank and as puja time was fast approaching he prayed to be helped in this misfortune. As a result of his prayer and by the special grace of the deity, a chank appeared in the tank. Then he placed a lingam before him and, with the help of the chank miraculously provided, performed his worship in an acceptable and proper manner. He also prayed that a chank might appear each day he should worship at this tank. The Puranas say that this request was granted and has been since continued until the present day. In this connection my informant remarks that it is to be noted that twelve ordinary years constitute one divine day.

Thousands of pilgrims resort to the Tirukalikundram shrines each year and the marvel of this story is one of the great assets of the place just as is the periodic liquefaction of blood to the shrine of San Gennario in Naples.

In temple worship, the chank fulfils important service. The ordinary and sinistral forms are both employed whenever the temple possesses them. The former is used in the menial duty of summoning the god's attention, announcing the commencement of the principal rites as well as in calling the devout to worship ; such are among the general explanations given for its employment, but some ethnologists hold that the innate and primitive significance of the use of the blowing chank in temple worship is to scare away hostile and evil-working spirits. This is a reasonable belief as there is little or no doubt that the chank was used originally as a horn or trumpet by tribes holding animistic beliefs prior to the development of the Brahman religion which appears to have adopted the use of the chank in religious ceremonies together with many other rites from the devil-fearing tribes who gradually came into the fold of the new and higher religious belief.

In this connection should be mentioned the custom which prevails largely in Bengal of keeping blowing chanks in the houses of the better class people for use in family worship. Mr. A. R. Banerji, I.C.S., the late Dewan of Cochin State, informs me that it is a general custom in Bengal to turn out with these shells during eclipses and earthquakes and to keep up a continuous blowing till the eclipse or earthquake be over.

A rather striking effect is produced when the chank is used in temple ritual as a sort of rhythmical accompaniment when it plays the part of kannagōlu or tālavinyāsa.[1]

In Hindu temples the four daily services take place before dawn, at noon, at sunset, and at 9 or 10 P.M. At these times the Ochchans, the caste entrusted solely in the Tamil country with the duty of chank-blowing in temples, announce the commencement of each service and punctuate the various rites with the drone of their shell according to the customary ritual. Among the Uriyas the corresponding caste of temple servants is that of the Rāvulos, whose caste duty is to sound the chank during services in Saivite temples when the god is being taken in procession as also to prepare garlands of flowers for the adornment of the god. Like the Ochchans, they are not usually whole-time servants of the temple, but while the former earn money as musicians at weddings, performing upon a long silver trumpet, the Rāvulos make and sell garlands to the laity. The Ochchans never use the chank except in the temples, whereas the Rāvulos are employed to sound it at Brahmans' weddings. It is a rule among the latter that they must possess at least two blowing chanks, lest, losing one, the temple service should suffer in consequence.

In Bengal, the Ramavat sect of Vaishnavas pay particular attention to the call of the chank. By them all forms of worship except the unceasing repetition of the name Rama or Hari are deemed useless, but in every ākhāra or monastery of the sect an idol is tended at regular hours to the sound of chank shells and gongs, while offerings of fruit and flowers are presented by the laity (Risley, II, p. 340).

Chanks to be used as wind instruments are chosen of as large size as procurable, often 8 inches long by 4 inches in diameter. The only preparation they require is to have the extreme apex removed, usually by hammering. No tune properly so called can be played, but the tone is capable of much modulation by the lips, and the long drawn notes as they drone clear and mellow on the evening breeze have a haunting charm that clings sweet and seductive in the memory ; it has a mystic wail perfect in appropriateness to its religious use before the shrines of the gods of a profoundly philosophical creed.

Sinistral shells whenever possessed by a temple, are usually mounted in handsomely decorated golden settings and used as libation vessels in the service of the god. Whether the god be Siva in the form of a lingam, or Vishnu or other deity represented in anthropomorphic shape, the officiating priests must lave it with water rendered sacred by being poured from the mouth of a chank.[2] On certain auspicious days cow's milk is used for libations in lieu of water. And if the doubly sacred sinistral chank is not possessed by the temple, then a choice example of the ordinary form must be used.

In family devotions the chank is also employed as a libation vessel by strictly devout Brahmans, both Saivites and Vaishnavites. Daily before the mid-day meal

[1] Day, "Music and Musical Instruments of S. India and the Deccan," 1891.

[2] A Tamil proverb says: "If you pour water into a chank it becomes holy water ; if you pour it into a pot, it remains merely water."

the Brahman head of the family, after taking his bath, prostrates himself before the family shrine and then, chanting some hymns from the Vedas, pours water over the image of the deity from the mouth of a chank shell. Then he dresses the god and commences his prayers.

In Thibet the call of the chank is amongst the most familiar sounds to be heard in the monasteries and temples of the Lamaistic faith. The writings of travellers in that most priest-ridden of countries, contain frequent mention of the custom. Sven Hedin for example, when describing the opening ceremonies of the Losar or new year festival which he saw in the great monastery of Tashilunpo in Shigatze—the seat of the Tashi Lama, says :—" Suddenly from the uppermost platforms on the roof ring out deep, long drawn-out blasts of horns over the country ; a couple of monks show themselves against the sky ; they blow on singular sea-shells, producing a penetrating sound, which is echoed back in shrill and yet heavy tones from the fissured rocks behind the convent ; they summon the Gelugpa, the brotherhood of yellow monks, to the festival."

Tea-drinking among the Lamas must never be missed ; the monks partake of it even in the midst of the most important ceremonies, and to prevent the terrible misfortune of a brother being too late for any distribution of tea, the departure of the novices from the kitchen bearing their loads of hot tea in large copper vessels on their shoulders, is signalled to all in the various halls and cells by a loud call upon a chank-horn from the temple roof.

Sven Hedin also describes (" Trans-Himalaya," Vol. II, p. 19) a cave inhabited by a hermit reputed to be one hundred years old, who passed his days crouching in a niche in the wall continually saying his prayers and occasionally blowing a faint blast on a chank.

And when a monk, no longer able to answer the shell's call to gather with his brethren round the teapots and the bowls of tsamba, passes quietly away, the same sound summons those who remain to attend his funeral mass.

In the purer Buddhism of Ceylon the chank cult also finds place, and figures prominently among the musical instruments employed to lend *éclat* to the periodic procession (*perahera*) of the tooth relic at Kandy.

(*b*)—BRANDING.

All Sri Vaishnavite Brahmans, irrespective of profession, are expected to undergo a ceremony of initiation into Vaishnavism after the Upanayanam ceremony of investment with the sacred thread, in the belief that it is the duty of all of their creed to carry throughout life a memorial of their god upon their person. To effect this, resort is had to branding with heated copper seals made in the conventional form of the various symbols of Vishnu.

Members of this sect are not compelled to undergo this ordeal more than once during their lifetime, but the Madhva sect which comprises chiefly Canarese-speaking Brahmans, have to submit to it as often as they visit their Guru. Men of other castes who become followers of a Vaishnava or a Madhva Achārya (Guru) are expected to present themselves before the Guru for the purpose of being branded. But the ceremony is optional and not compulsory as in the case of a Brahman. Even the women in Vaishnavite families must submit to this branding; in their case it takes place after marriage in the case of Sri Vaishnavites, while among the Madhvas one form of branding should be performed at any age before marriage should the Guru visit the neighbourhood, and a more formal one again after marriage. Regarding Sri Vaishnavites, Thurston (I, 370) states that "the disciples after a purificatory bath and worship of their gods, proceed to the residence of the Achārya, or to the mutt where they are initiated into their religion, and branded with the chakra on the right shoulder and with the chank on the left. The initiation consists in imparting to the disciple, in a very low tone, the Mūla Mantram, the word Nāmonarā-yanāya, the sacred syllable Ōm, and a few mantrams from the Brahma Rahasyam (Secrets about God). A person who has not been initiated thus is regarded as unfit to take part in the ceremonies which have to be performed by Brahmans. Even close relations, if orthodox, will refuse to take food prepared or touched by the uninitiated."

As Vaishnavite Gurus are few in number, it is necessary for them to peregrinate the country, halting at suitable centres to brand those of their followers living in the neighbourhood just as a Bishop in certain Christian churches tours his diocese to afford confirmation (*i.e.*, initiation) services at periodical intervals. In populous districts where Vaishnavites are in numerical strength the scene at each of the Guru's halting places is intense with interest. Thousands of his disciples gather round eager to be branded. Brahmans are there in force, but men of many other castes and even Paraiyans are there. The ceremonies begin by the making of a fire in a mud pot (*homa kunda*), accompanied by the chant of hymns and the offering of prayer to Vishnu. As Brahmans present themselves for the rite the Guru lifts the copper brands which have been heating meanwhile in the fire and applies them to the shoulders of the people, the chakra on the right and the chank on the left. As each stamp is made the Guru's assistant, usually a Dasari or Vaishnavite mendicant, smears the burnt spots with a paste of *namakkatti*, the same white clay used by Vaishnavites when painting the *namam* or sect mark (improperly called caste mark) on their forehead.

Paraiyans and low caste disciples may not be branded directly by the Guru; in their case he heats the instruments and hands them to the Dasari, his assistant, who performs the actual operation.

With regard to the branding customs of Madhva Vaishnavites, who believe that to carry a lasting outward and visible sign of their deity on their body helps them to obtain salvation through him, Thurston (I, pp. 371-373) supplies an interesting account:—" Madhvas have four mutts to which they repair for the branding ceremony, viz., Vayasaraya, Sumathendra, and Mulabagal in Mysore, and Uttaraja in South Canara. The followers of the Uttaraja mutt are branded in five places in the case of adult males, and boys after the thread investiture. The situations and emblems selected are the chakra on the right upper arm, right side of the chest, and above the navel; the chank on the left shoulder and left side of the chest. Women and girls after marriage, are branded with the chakra on the right forearm, and the chank on the left. In the case of widows, the marks are impressed on the shoulders as in the case of males. The disciples of the three other mutts are generally branded with the chakra on the right upper arm, and chank on the left. As the branding is supposed to remove sins committed during the interval, they get it done every time they see their Guru. There is with Madhvas no restriction as to the age at which the ceremony should be performed. Even a new-born babe, after the pollution period of ten days, must receive the mark of the chakra, if the Guru should turn up. Boys before the upanayanam, and girls before marriage are branded with the chakra on the abdomen just above the navel. The copper or brass branding instruments (mudras) are not heated to a very high temperature, but sufficient to singe the skin, and leave a deep black mark in the case of adults, and a light mark in that of young people and babies. In some cases, disciples who are afraid of being hurt, bribe the person who heats the instruments; but as a rule, the Guru regulates the temperature so as to suit the individual. If, for example, the disciple is a strong well-built man, the instruments are well heated, and, if he is a weakling, they are allowed to cool somewhat before their application. If the operator has to deal with babies, he presses the instrument against a wet rag before applying it to the infant's skin. Some Matathipathis (head priests of the mutt) are, it is said, inclined to be vindictive, and to make a very hot application of the instruments if the disciple has not paid the fee (guru-kānika) to his satisfaction. The fee is not fixed in the case of Sri Vaishnavas, whereas Madhvas are expected to pay from one to three months' income for being branded. Failure to pay is punished with excommunication on some pretext or other. The area of skin branded generally peels off within a week, leaving a pale mark of the mudra, which either disappears in a few months, or persists throughout life. Madhvas should stamp mudras with gopi paste[1] daily on various parts of the body. The names of these mudras are chakra, chank or sankha, gātha (the weapon of war used by Bhima, one of the Pāndavas), padma (lotus), and Narāyana. The chakra is stamped thrice on the abdomen above the navel, twice on the right flank, twice on the right side of the chest above the nipple, twice on the right arm, once on the right temple, once on the left side of the chest, and once on the left arm. The chank is stamped twice on the right side of the chest, in two places on the left arm, and once on the left temple. The gātha is stamped in two places on the right arm, twice on the chest, and in one spot on the forehead. The padma is stamped twice on the left arm, and twice on the left side of the chest. Narāyana is stamped on all places where other mudra marks have been made.

[1] Properly *gopi chandiram*, a paste made of white kaolin mixed with sandalwood.

Sometimes it is difficult to put on all the marks after the daily morning bath. In such cases, a single mudra mark, containing all the five mudras, is made to suffice. Some regard the chakra mudra as sufficient on occasions of emergency."

So far as I can learn the branding instruments which are employed to sear the two chief symbols, chank and chakra, by means of heat are usually made of copper. In other localities brands of different metals appear to be used as Risley (II, p. 339) states that the Rāmānuja, a Vaishnavite sect in Bengal, when undergoing the initiatory rite (*tapta-mudra*) are branded with the chakra on the right shoulder and the chank on the left, by means of a brand made of eight metals (ashta-dhatū)—gold, silver, copper, brass, tin, lead, iron, and zinc.

Various deviations from the standard ceremonial exist in certain districts; among these is that followed by the Bedar or Boya caste of the Southern Deccan, a caste which largely constituted the old fighting stock of this district. Among them the men are branded on the shoulders by the priest of a Hanuman shrine with the sign of the chank and of the chakra, in the belief that this will enable them to go to swarga (heaven). Female Bedars who are branded become Basavis (temple women) and are dedicated to a male deity and called Gandu Basavis or male Basavis (Thurston, I, p. 194).

This branding of temple girls, or Dēva-dāsi as they are termed in the Tamil country, with symbols of the chank and chakra is always an essential feature in the ceremonies which mark their dedication to the god of their temple, whom thenceforward they serve with dance and song.

Allied to branding is tattooing. The Tandans of Malabar, a caste about the level of the Tiyyans, adopt this method to show devotion to the deity, and among the religious symbols worked into the skin of their arms is that of the chank (Thurston, VII, 10).

(*c*) THE MENDICANT'S CONCH.

Beggars throughout India occasionally use the chank shell as a musical instrument, and with certain castes of religious mendicants it is an essential part of their professional paraphernalia, so much so that a Tamil proverb likens things in continual association to " the breech of the chank and the mouth of the mendicant."

The Dasari, who belongs to a caste of Vaishnavite mendicants well represented in the Madras Presidency, is often seen in North Arcot and the Southern Deccan, announcing his arrival in a village by blasts on the chank-shell which in that part of the country is one of his five insignia. In Telugu districts the Dasaris are more secular and less religious, and the caste is known as Sanku Dāsari or vulgarly Sanku jadi, the chank-blowing caste.

A mendicant's conch sometimes has the apical orifice mounted in brass; temple conchs are usually without any ornamentation, but the Udipi temple owns one very handsomely mounted in brass and this is sounded whenever the god (Krishna) is carried in procession in the temple car.

(*d*) DEDICATION OF TEMPLES AND HOUSES.

Wherever a new temple is built, or when a new shrine or god is established and added to the number already there, its dedicatory ceremonies include as one of the most important a special libation to the god from the mouths of 108 chanks, or better still, from 1,008 chanks if so many can be afforded, filled with water and flowers.

The building of an ordinary house in the Tamil country must also have its ceremonial dedication at the time the foundation trenches are dug, though among low caste people the rite consists merely of a superstitious act to ensure good luck or to baulk the evil eye. It is carried out with the help of the sacred chank which thus is seen to touch the lives of the people at every point from the cradle to the grave. Before a single stone in the foundation is laid, the ceremony is carried out on a day carefully chosen as being highly auspicious. A chank is then buried beneath the first stone laid. An old reference to this occurs in a petition quoted by Wheeler (*fide* Thurston, III, p. 147) from two natives of Madras, in connection with the founding of a village called Chintadrepettah, now a populous division of Madras City. The entry runs :—" Expended towards digging a foundation where chanks were buried with accustomary ceremonies." Roman Catholic converts from low castes follow this custom, as well as Hindus ; in Tuticorin, if a Roman Catholic Parayan desires to build a house, the carpenter employed by him chooses an auspicious day by reference to a native calendar, a chank is bought in the bazaar and on the day chosen, having dug a foundation trench and prepared at the bottom a bed of coral stone and mortar, the chank is laid thereon. In the cavity of the shell small fragments of five metals (panjalokam), gold, silver, copper, iron and lead, are placed, turmeric and sandalwood water is sprinkled over, and then the whole is hidden under a mass of sweet-smelling flowers. The ceremony is ended ; the first stone may now be lowered into place upon the chank and its contents, and good luck is believed to be assured to him who will inhabit the house.

It may, however, happen that in spite of every precaution, an inauspicious site appears to have been chosen as shown by a sequence of misfortunes happening to the householder. In such cases Hindus may perform a special ceremony called Chank-usthabanam to remedy the evil. A chank-shell is filled with water and incantations made for forty-five days. At the end of this period of propitiation, the chank is buried under the house wall. (Winslow, " Tamil and English Dictionary," p. 390, Madras 1862.)

Among the Parawa caste living in Tuticorin and other coast towns and villages in Tinnevelly and Rāmnād, misfortune is often sought to be averted from the individual by almost completely burying a chank shell in the floor of the hall (*kūdam*), about two feet on the inner side of the doorway to the street. A small portion of the back of the shell shows as a patch of white on the surface of the floor. The explanation of the custom current among Parawas is that the shell is so placed that when an inmate leaves the house, he must pass over it, usually touching it, and this will prevent misfortune happening to him.

(e) MARRIAGE CEREMONIES.

The chank has important but variable functions to perform at weddings among all Hindu non-Brahman castes in the districts of the south of India, where this shell is blown by the barber (ambattan) particularly at or immediately after the tying of the *tali* or marriage badge around the bride's neck; the bridal couple usually occupy a raised platform, and round and round this the barber walks while blowing his chank. In Bengal this custom of chank-blowing during weddings is even more general; a common formula which runs

> "Ganga ka pani samundra ki sank
> Bar kanya jag jag anand."
>
> ("May Ganges water and sea-chank betide
> Enduring bliss to bridegroom and bride.")

is usually recited during the marriage (Risley, II, p. 116) with reference to the blasts on the conch which accompany the ceremonies—the equivalent of the marriage bells in Christian ritual.

In Telugu districts the chank is not used by any caste, non-Brahman as well as Brahman, during weddings, as this is considered inauspicious because chank-blowing is specially associated with funeral ceremonies.

Usually a man of a special caste is engaged to blow the chank at the customary times; in the Tamil country the caste barbers (ambattans) perform this duty; among the Telugus the chank blower is usually a Dasari, among the Uriyas, a Ravulo.

Sometimes, however, women of the family or of the caste perform the chank-blowing duty. Among Bengal Brahmans, for instance, one section of the elaborate and lengthy marriage ceremonies consists of a procession of seven married ladies headed by the bride's mother going round the bridegroom seven times, some sprinkling libations of water and vociferating the hymeneal cry of *ulu-ulu*. One of the seven carries a conch and blows it as she goes (Risley, I, p. 150). A custom somewhat akin to the above prevails among the Kallan caste of Tanjore, Madura, Trichinopoly and Tinnevelly. On the wedding day the sister of the bridegroom goes to the house of the bride, accompanied by women, some of whom carry flowers, coconuts, paddy, turmeric, milk, ghee, etc. On the way two of these women blow chank shells. (Thurston, III, p. 80.)

In passing it is interesting to note that a section of this caste, the Puramalai nādu Kallans, practise the rite of circumcision probably as a survival of a forgotten forcible conversion to Muhammadanism. The rite is carried out in a grove or plain outside the village and *en route* to the place, and throughout the ceremony a chank is blown at frequent intervals. (Thurston, III, p. 74.)

It is noteworthy that Brahmans in the Tamil and Telugu districts do not employ the chank during marriage ceremonies though their brethren in Bengal do. Among Telugu Brahmans living in Uriya districts the custom of Bengal used to be followed at marriages, but this is gradually dying out; as one Brahman in Berhampur (Ganjām) remarked "The present day Brahmans here have more regard for the magic flute than for the divine voice issuing from the chank."

In Bengal the association of the chank with marriage is more intimate and deep than elsewhere; no Bengali lady is properly or legally married unless chank bangles, which should be lacquered red, be placed upon her wrists. In the Madras Presidency, marriage bangles are used only by a few sections of the agricultural and pastoral castes (Vellalans and Idaiyans).

One of the most interesting facts brought to light during the present research is the weighty evidence we have that in former days the tali, the essential marriage symbol among Tamils, was directly connected with the chank, either composed of a piece of the shell or of a metal ornament in the form of a miniature chank shell. We find this marriage badge named specifically *sankhu tali* among four castes widely separated both geographically and in status and civilisation. First are the *Chanku tali Vellalans*, a section of the great Vellalar caste, who wear, according to Winslow ("Tamil and English Dictionary," Madras, 1862), a representation of the chank on either side of a central symbol. Unfortunately, apart from this reference, I have been unable to trace the location of these Vellalans at the present day, or to obtain any details of the custom.

Two other castes with the same marriage badge occur on the West Coast, and it is significant that one is undoubtedly of Tamil origin. This is an immigrant branch of the Idaiyans known locally as Puvandans, settled in Travancore. On ceremonial occasions the women wear the Tamil Idaiyan dress while in ordinary life they attire themselves after the fashion of Nayar women. Their tali is known as *sankhu tali* and a small ornament in the form of a chank is its most conspicuous feature. (Thurston, II, 366.)

The other West Coast caste using a *sankhu tali* is that of the Thandan Pulayans, a small division of the Pulayans who dwell in South Malabar and Cochin. The women dress in a leaf skirt made from the stems of a sedge called *thanda*, which are cut into equal lengths, woven at one end and tied round the waist so that they hang down below the knees.

According to Ananthakrishna Aiyar (Thurston, VII, p. 23.): "At the marriage ceremony, the tāli (marriage badge) is made of a piece of a conch shell (*Turbinella rapa*) which is tied on the bride's neck at an auspicious hour. She is taken before her landlord, who gives her some paddy, and all the coconuts on the tree beneath which she happens to kneel. . . . . . . To ascertain whether a marriage will be a happy one, a conch shell is spun round. If it falls to the north, it predicts good fortune; if to the east or west, the omens are favourable; if to the south, very unfavourable."

Lastly, and most interesting of all, we find a caste calling their marriage badge *sankhu tali*, which on examination shows no likeness to a chank shell. These are the Parawas of the coast towns on the Indian side of the Gulf of Mannar. When the Portuguese arrived there early in the sixteenth century, these people, who were principally pearl fishers, chank divers, and fishermen, were orthodox Hindus, but the stress of Muhammadan competition drove them into alliance with the Portuguese and they went over in a body to the Roman Catholic church. To-day the badge tied around the bride's neck on marriage consists of three ornaments, a central cross flanked on either side by the symbol of the Holy Ghost; nevertheless it is called *sankhu tali* as among the castes first mentioned. There is no doubt that when the caste was a Hindu one the *tali* was true to name, indeed Parawa tradition is definite, for it asserts that originally the central ornament was a small figure of some Hindu God (probably Krishna) flanked by one of a chank shell on each side. The use of the original name is a strange persistence in view of nearly 400 years' sojourn within the Christian fold; it is one of the many signs of tolerance shown by the Roman Catholic priesthood towards their converts' prejudices on immaterial points—a tolerance in petty matters that has done much to help that church in its propaganda.

Among some castes, including the Bauris and Dandasis of Ganjām, turmeric water from a chank shell is poured seven times over the hands of bride and bridegroom, which are tied together with seven turns of a turmeric-dyed thread. (Thurston, Vols. I. and II.)

(*f*) DEATH CEREMONIES.

Throughout the Tamil country all non-Brahman castes which observe Hindu rites have the chank sounded as the body is being taken to the funeral pyre or to the burial ground. It is usual also to employ the conch-blower on the last day of the sraddh ceremonies in those castes which follow the orthodox ritual. Among the Telugus these same rites are largely followed, but it is said that Vaishnavites do not observe them. Among both races, the Brahmans do not have the conch blown at any period of the obsequies—a sign that lends weight to the theory that the chank has been borrowed by Brahmanism from another religion.

In the Madura and Tinnevelly districts the conch-blowers at a funeral are Ambattans or barbers, the same caste as performs likewise at weddings. Among the Idaiyans of these and the neighbouring districts one part of the funeral rites consists in the son perambulating the pyre thrice with a pot of water on his shoulder; at each turn the barber makes a hole in it with a shell when the head of the corpse is reached. Finally the pot is broken near the head. (Thurston, II, p. 362.)

Further north, in the East Coast districts from Tanjore and Salem to the Kistna River, the Panisavans are by caste custom the funeral conch-blowers; they may indeed be accounted the undertaker caste, as it is their duty to carry news of the death to the relations of the deceased. It is they who generally keep all the materials necessary for the funeral including the palanquin required for the conveyance of the corpse to the cremation ground. At the funeral, the Panisavan follows the corpse, blowing his conch. When the son goes round the corpse with a pot of water, the Panisavan accompanies him sounding his conch the while. On the last day of the death ceremonies (Karmandhiram) the Pansivan should also be present and blow his conch especially when the tali is removed from the widow's neck. (Thurston, VI, p. 56.)

The insignia of the Panisavans are the chank and the tharai, a long straight trumpet.

In Coimbatore district, the duty of sounding the death conch belongs to the members of an important sub-division of Paraiyans, called on this account, Sankhu Paraiyan. (Thurston, VI, p. 81.) In Travancore when a headman or kaikkaran of the Paraiyans settled there happens to die, a chank-shell is buried with the corpse. (Thurston, VI, p. 134.)

The chank sometimes has a place in the death ceremonies of castes which are not Hinduised. Thus among the Cherumans of Malabar and Cochin, a caste of agricultural serfs, according to Mr. Ananthakrishna Aiyar (Thurston, II, p. 81.), "The son or nephew is the chief mourner, who erects a mound of earth on the south side of the hut, and uses it as a place of worship. For seven days, both morning and evening, he prostrates himself before it, and sprinkles the water of a tender coconut on it. On the eighth day, his relatives, friends, the Vallon, and the devil-driver assemble together. The devil-driver turns round and blows his conch, and finds out the position of the ghost, whether it has taken up its abode in the mound, or is kept under restraint by some deity. Should the latter be the case, the ceremony of deliverance has to be performed, after which the spirit is set up as a household deity."

How far the conch is used in funeral rites outside the Madras Presidency, I am not in a position to say, except in regard to Thibet, where as already incidentally mentioned, it is a custom to sound it as the body of a monk or a nun is being conveyed from the place where death occurred.

(*g*) TOTEMS.

Totems as the distinctive signs of exogamous septs must have been at one time universal among tribes of Dravidian origin. To-day a well developed totemistic system characterises the tribal organisation of the Santals and Oraons who retain languages distinct from those of the surrounding peoples, know nothing of the caste system, and who continue to worship non-Aryan gods. Among the Santals 91 septs are known, and one of these is known as Sankh. The members of this sept may not cut, burn, nor use the shell, nor may the women of this sept wear it in personal adornment.

Above these still primitive tribes and between them and the fully Hinduised peoples who are split up into castes, are a large number of partially Hinduised tribes which in many cases show distinct traces of a totemistic organisation. Among these the

Kurmis of Bengal, and the nomad Koravas who wander throughout the peninsular part of India, both have an exogamous sept or gotra of which the totem is the chank-shell. Among the Kurmis this sept is called Sankhawar; its members are prohibited from wearing ornaments made from chank-shells. With the Koravas it is termed Samudrāla, signifying the sea, and people of this sept may not use the chank in any way. Higher than these are the Kalinjis, an Uriya agricultural caste, and the Kurubas, a caste of shepherds and weavers widely spread throughout the Madras Presidency. Both castes comprise septs named after the chank, in the case of the Kalinjis, Sankho, in that of the Kurubas, Sankhu. I am not aware whether the septs among the former caste have now totemistic value, or if it has become merely a name, a gotra name; in any case it may be taken as certain that in the pre-Hinduised condition, the name of the gotra was of real totemistic value. Bhāgo (tiger) and nāgo (cobra) are names of two other gotras of obviously totemistic origin. With the Kurubas, the sept is undoubtedly exogamous and its totemistic character certain.

Another caste or sub-caste showing by the names of its sections a probable totemistic origin is that of the Koppala or Toththala, a sub-division of the Velamas, a caste of agriculturists in the Vizagapatam district. Among their sections are some named Nāga (cobra), Sankha (chank), Tulasi (basil or tulsi) and Tāblēu (tortoise). At the present day these divisions although apparently of totemistic origin, have no significance so far as marriage is concerned. (Thurston, VII, p. 340.)

(*h*) EVIL-EYE SUPERSTITIONS.

Belief in the reality of the malign results which ensue from being overlooked by the evil-eye is frequently present in an acute form in the Madras Presidency. It is specially dreaded in the case of houses under construction and in respect to valued cattle. Everywhere in Tamil districts the custom prevails more or less extensively of seeking protection for draft bullocks by tying a small chank-shell upon the forehead of such as are in good condition or in any way specially valuable or beautiful in their owner's eyes. Of late years the custom has tended to fall into abeyance in certain districts. As is to be expected the people of country villages cling to it with greater tenacity than those in towns. Many, however, decorate their bulls in this way without thought of it as an amulet against evil—to them it is merely an old custom to be followed, or else they put it on their favourite animals as an ornament to mark the pride they have in them. Again, some, from a peculiar shyness often met when discussing such matters with the peasantry, deny that the chank-shell is used as an amulet although in reality it may be so used by them.

In the southern Deccan the custom appears to be falling more quickly into abeyance than in Tamil districts. The Collector of Kurnul informs me that though the practice survives in parts of Dhone, Kumbum, Koilkuntla and Sirvel taluks of tying a chank on the forehead or round the necks of bullocks and ponies, it is gradually dying out; in Bellary the Collector states that it still prevails in Bellary, Hospet and Hadagalli taluks in respect to bullocks, but adds that the people do not now attach any religious or secular significance to it. In Anantapur the Collector states that the custom is not now followed in that district.

In Madras City it is quite common to see it and there also I have seen a shell hung by a chain or a cord round the neck of a cow-buffalo when in milk to prevent her being "overlooked" and her milk thereby dried up prematurely. In country villages this latter custom is not infrequent both in regard to ordinary cows and to cow-buffaloes. In the Madura, Trichinopoly, Salem and adjacent districts a shell is often hung round the necks of jutka and pack ponies, not only by Hindu owners, but also by Muhammadans. In Madura specially valued sheep occasionally are similarly guarded from evil, and in the same district I have seen milch-goats protected in a like manner. In all these cases the shells used are of small size, the great majority being dead or sub-fossil shells from the mud-beds of Ceylon. They are the same as are sold as feeding spouts for infants in every Tamil bazaar. A hole is bored or broken in the back and the rope passed through this and out at the mouth of the shell. The surface is generally roughly engraved in a coarse spiral or scroll pattern.

Used probably for a similar purpose may have been the handsomely engraved large chank shell obtained from an oblong sarcophagus of red pottery found in the prehistoric burial site at Perambair in the south of Chingleput district. The size is much greater than any I have ever seen used to decorate ordinary cattle; no ordinary person owned it we may be certain—probably it decorated the forehead of a bull or possibly of an elephant belonging to a man of great local importance. From the same tombs came three other handsomely decorated chank ornaments, two of which were probably ornaments for the hair (see p. 41 for further particulars).

Once only have I seen[1] more than a single shell hung round the neck of any animal, but that in ancient times a different habit at least occasionally prevailed is possible, to judge from the string of 16 small chank shells from a barrow near Guntakal junction in the Anantapur district, now to be seen in Madras Museum. All these shells have had the apices broken in and partly rubbed down and each has the thickest part of the body perforated from side to side so permitting them to be strung together. They appear to have formed a necklace, but whether they were suspended round the neck of a bull or may be hung like a chain of office round the neck of some person of importance, we have no means of determining.

In Malabar the chank is little in evidence, but Logan ("Malabar Manual," 1887, Vol. I, p. 175) records a belief there prevalent that a cow will stop giving milk unless a shell (not necessarily a chank) is tied conspicuously about her horns and at Tanur, Malabar, I have seen valuable sheep with shells other than chanks hung round the neck.

[1] At Tirupalakudi, on Palk Strait.

Further north, in the coast villages of South Canara, south of Mangalore, rings made from Strombus shells but known locally as chank rings are employed by parents to avert the evil eye from their young children. At Kasargod, Bekal and the adjacent villages I have found the custom especially common among the Mukuvans, a caste of immigrant Malayali fishermen. Children from 3 to 4 years old in these villages are frequently given necklaces made of Strombus rings alternating with elongated glass beads. Some other castes in the same neighbourhood, Mokayans and Tiyyans together with some Mappillas, are said to follow the same custom. Usually the rings do not exceed twelve in each necklace. Adults do not wear these amulets as is the habit of the woman of certain sections of the Cheruman caste in Malabar (*cf.* p. 39) and of the Hill Vedans of Travancore. How far these and other facts connote former wide or even universal prevalence of this habit among the indigenous population of Malabar, is a line of inquiry likely to repay careful investigation.

Finger rings purporting to be made from chank shells, but usually cut from a small species of *Strombus* common on the western coast of the Gulf of Mannar, are also used very freely throughout the Tamil country and also in Malabar and Cochin, chiefly by non-Brahmans among Hindus, as amulets against evil spirits, the evil eye and certain sicknesses. In Tinnevelly, Madura and Rāmnād the custom is very prevalent among both sexes of non-Brahmans. Labbai and Marakkayar Muhammadans in whose veins much Hindu blood is present, also affect the custom. The Vellalans, although like Brahman adults, they wear, except in one section, neither chank-bangles nor rings, often provide their children with chank-rings or else with pieces of chank-shell tied on the wrist of the right hand by means of black thread, as an amulet against the disease called chedi which is, I believe, rickets. In some cases the ring or piece of chank is placed on the wrist only when the disease has laid hold of the child, in others it is tied on when the child attains its second month and kept there till it is three years old, when it is believed that all danger of contracting the disease has passed. Among the castes ranking next—Chettis, Kollans, Thachchans, Thattans, Naidus, Idaiyans, and Chaluppans, a chank-ring is often worn as an amulet against pimples on the face; occasionally their young children are provided with small and roughly ornamented chank-bangles to safeguard them against *chedi*. The low castes or Panchamas such as Pallans, Vallayans, Paraiyans, etc., are the most regular devotees of these amulets.

The Roman Catholic Parawas of Tuticorin and the other Parawa strongholds on the Pescaria Coast have also been great believers in the virtue of chank amulets, and till recently all babies were given chank-bangles to protect from convulsions and from *chedi*. Even now the poorer and more ignorant continue to employ these amulets, keeping them on the wrists for about three years. The richer and better educated have either abandoned the practice or keep the bangles on for a much abbreviated period. The Parawas formerly also employed pieces of the curious egg-capsule of the chank for the same purpose as the bangle, a fragment of the capsule (*chanku-pu*, literally "chank-flower") being tied by means of thread upon babies' wrists.

In Madura chank amulets are used even more freely than in Tinnevelly. In addition to bangles and rings used as amulets against the evil eye, or ailments such as *chedi* and pimples, very roughly fashioned and imperfectly rounded fragments of chank shells are used in the manner of beads to make necklaces which are used as amulets. Maravans, Paraiyans, and Chakkiliyans are among the castes chiefly addicted to the wearing of these and other chank amulets; these people often give their children both chank-bangles and necklaces of chank-beads with a view to multiplying the countervailing influences against the evil eye and against disease.

Chank-bead necklaces (*chanku malai*) are also worn largely by children of the poorer Chettis and of the Vanniyans (oilmongers) who, though they do not generally wear chank-bangles, will wear these chank-bead necklaces. The people of the lower castes also use the same rough beads to make bracelets (*chanku pasi*) worn on the wrists for the same object as the bead necklaces. Similar customs in regard to rings and bead necklaces prevail in Tanjore and in South Arcot, where the low castes, especially Vanniyans, Koravans, Paraiyans, Chakkiliyans and wandering Lambadis, generally wear them as amulets against evil spirits, the evil eye and sickness. Koratti women appear to be the only ones in South Arcot who wear bead bracelets in addition to other bangles according to information kindly supplied by the Collector, Mr. Azizuddin.

The trade in these amulets is of considerable dimensions. Thus the Tahsildar of Chidambaram reports that rings worth about Rs. 500 are sold yearly in his taluk to the residents and to the thousands of devotees who flock to the great temple of Nataraja. The price runs from two pies to one anna per ring—some are very rough untrimmed *Strombus* rings, while the higher priced may be of real chank with a few oblique lines of ornament sawed or filed on the outer surface.

The rough beads used in making necklaces and bracelets look very much like tiny carpal bones; they sell about eight beads for one pie—a whole necklace may be bought for one anna; the small bangles worn by babies in Madura and Tinnevelly cost 3 to 5 annas per pair. The latter are made largely in Kilakarai, a large Muhammadan settlement on the Rāmnād coast, near the head of the Gulf of Mannar. The majority are cut chiefly from under-sized shells too small to have any value in the Bengal market. By rights these shells should not be fished; they should be put back alive by the divers in order to grow to adult dimensions. This precaution is followed as far as circumstances permit in the Tuticorin chank fishery which is conducted departmentally by the Government of Madras; in the Rāmnād fishery the short-sighted greed of the renter and his employees takes no account of any such precaution for the future prosperity of the fishery.

(*i*) For personal adornment.

In personal adornment, and apart from any uses it is put to in the form of amulets, the chank-shell is employed principally as the crude material wherefrom beautiful bracelets of many patterns are made for use in Bengal and the adjoining provinces; subsidiary uses to which it is put are to fashion from it finger rings, necklaces, disc ornaments for headdresses and caps, and as a recent addition, coat and dress buttons.

The bangle industry in all phases is treated separately and at full length in Section II, to which the reader is referred for details.

Rings actually made from chank-shell are not manufactured in any quantity; their place is taken largely by those made from a much smaller shell, a species of *Strombus*, found on the Rāmnād coast of the Gulf of Mannar. So far as I can learn, the industry is localised at Kilakarai, a seaport of Rāmnād inhabited largely by Muhammadan (Labbai) fishermen, pearl-fishers and chank-divers. The rings are usually exported with a minimum of finish; only the roughness of the edge is rubbed off and nearly always the chestnut stippling is clearly recognisable. Many are sold in the bazaars or by peddlers throughout the Tamil and Malayalam districts, usually as amulets against the evil eye and against such minor ailments as pimples on the face and various skin troubles. So far as I can ascertain, the only people who use these rings in personal adornment are two tribes of low civilisation living in the Malayalam country—the Hill Vedans of Travancore and certain sections of the Cheruman tribe in Cochin and Malabar. The former I have not seen. They are described by Thurston (VI, p. 333) as living in wretched huts and employed chiefly as rice-field watchmen. He states that both the men and women of this tribe wear numerous bead necklaces interstrung or otherwise associated with a few of these rings. In a photograph given by the same authority (Vol. III, p. 177), a man is shown wearing numerous strings of glass beads passed *through* eight Strombus rings. In the case of the women these necklaces hang down as far as the abdomen.

The Cherumans were formerly the agrestic serfs of Malabar, Cochin and Travancore—the Malayalam country or Kerala. To-day they still remain largely in a servile condition, carrying on for their masters the heavy labour of the fields; they receive their pay almost always in kind. They are divided into a considerable number of endogamous sections differing in appellation in different districts—a sign of long-continued residence in a country of difficult intercommunication.

All Cheruman women are greatly addicted to the use of necklaces, particularly of the showy strings of beads now put within the reach of the poorest by the enterprise of Austrian and Italian manufacturers. Of other clothing they wear the scantiest—a very dirty, once white cloth, pendant from the waist, being their usual garb. Certain sections wear as a distinctive badge, in addition to numerous bead necklaces, a long cord whereon are strung large numbers of Strombus rings (*chanku modiram*)—they believe

[Photo by J. Hornell.

Fig. 1.—Group of Cheruman women wearing necklaces of so-called chank-rings.

[Photo by Vividha Kala Mandir.

Fig. 2.—Selling chank shells to pilgrims returning from Bét.

them to be of chank-shell. The bead necklaces are usually wound many times round the neck itself, roughly forming a collar often reaching as high as the chin. The chank necklace is worn at a lower level, and lies on the shoulders and on the upper part of the breast; it looks much like a chain of office and is indeed the badge of the tribal sept. At Tanur (Malabar) where after much trouble three Cheruman women were got together for my inspection, one of the husbands had to be paid a day's wages to keep guard over them to prevent their flight. They were all exceedingly shy, and it was with much reluctance that they stood up in front of my camera. As will be seen by reference to Pl. III, Fig. 1, the chank ring necklaces (*chanku modira mala*) are made up of a very large number of rings not strung but tied by the upper edge to a strong cord in such a way that each ring overlaps its neighbour on one side and is similarly overlapped on the other side by the succeeding ring, much as the rings in chain armour are arranged. From 50 to 100 rings are required to form a full necklace of this pattern; as each ring costs from 3 to 6 pies in the local bazaar, the total cost may amount to Re. 1-8-0 or Rs. 2, a large sum to these exceedingly poor people. The Cherumans who wear these chank chains in the Tanur neighbourhood say they belong to a sept named Kallādi Cherumans and that they wear them to distinguish themselves from the Paliya and other septs with which they may not intermarry. In Tanur bazaar I saw a single example of another pattern of this strange necklace worn by a woman also said to be a Kallādi Cheruman. In this case the number of rings used were comparatively few, 20 in all, and between each pair were strung a couple of glass beads of different colours. Each ring was separated by an interval of about an inch from its neighbour on either side, and instead of being fastened to the common cord by a single loop, it was fastened by two separate loops which enabled it to lie flat upon the skin. The woman shrank against the wall, averting her face and trying to sidle away, and it was with great difficulty she could be persuaded to answer a few particulars. Among other information she gave, was the statement that this necklet is believed to protect from evil spirits.

So far as I have been able to ascertain, these chank necklaces are assumed soon after a girl attains puberty if her parents can afford it. If they be very poor and cannot afford it, then, when her marriage is arranged, it is generally settled that the bride-groom shall provide the needful ornament. There is no special ceremony followed at the time a girl puts on her chank necklet for the first time. As a rule the men of the family attach the rings to the cord.

This custom seems to be losing ground quickly, for while many people knew of it further south in Malabar, I never saw this ornament in use in North Malabar. Many Cherumans were seen between Cannanore and Mount Dilly, but all said few use it now, preferring glass or imitation coral beads for their necklets. There is no doubt that formerly the custom was widely spread among the servile population of Kerala, and as these people's religious beliefs consist almost solely of the dread of malignant spirits, it is extremely probable that originally the necklet was used as an amulet against demons and the evil eye, though now it is more generally considered as a sept badge. The custom of long-settled Malayali immigrants (Mukuvans, etc.) on the South Canara coast, of putting similar necklaces round their children's necks already referred to on p. 36, appears to furnish strong corroboration of this conclusion.

In Bengal a few ornamental finger rings are now made, carved in simple patterns and highly polished. These are not in great demand, and I am uncertain as to whether they are worn as ornaments or as amulets. At Kilakarai a few roughly decorated thin finger-rings to be used as amulets are also produced, in addition to the roughly made, thick and clumsy sections cut from Strombus shells.

The first mention of the use of discs cut from chank-shells to ornament caps and headdresses occurs in Tavernier's "Indian Travels." In 1666 he was in Dacca and records the fact that Bhutan merchants took home quantities of "round and square pieces (of shell) of the size of our 15 sol coins." He also states that "all the people of the north, men, women, girls and boys, suspend small pieces of shell both round and square from their hair and ears."

Whether the trade is as large as in former days, I cannot say. It is now of small monetary value.

The Nagas of Assam, lately brought to prominent notice through the good work they did as carriers during the Abor punitive expedition (1912), employ these discs both to form necklaces and to decorate the handsome plaited cane helmets worn by the men. These latter are conical in shape, about a foot high, and covered with a layer of fur and hair, black or red in colour. When decorated with chank-shell discs, these are arranged as coronals, adding most effectively to the general design (W. Crooke, "Natives of Northern India," p. 47, London, 1907). As the Nagas are known to have set much greater store by the chank in former times, say prior to the middle of the nineteenth century, it is probable that then the use of chank discs as items of ornament was much more general among this race than it is now. Still the custom is quite common, for Mr. Stanley Kemp, who accompanied the Abor expedition as naturalist, informs me that the Naga coolies employed as carriers frequently wore necklaces formed of square concave portions of chank-shell with a large cornelian set *en cabochon* in the centre. Sometimes long cylindrical beads made from chank shell, tapered slightly at either end, were used instead and cornelian beads were often seen in conjunction.

In the middle of last century Major John Butler mentions ("Travels and Adventures in the Province of Assam," p. 148, London, 1855) that at sixteen years of age a Naga youth "puts on ivory armlets or else wooden or red-coloured cane ones round his neck. He suspends conch shells with a black thread" (round his neck) "puts brass ornaments into his ears and wears the black kilt; and if a man has killed another in war he wears three or four rows of cowries round the kilt." From a specimen of chank-shell necklace from the Naga hills contained in the ethnological collection of the Indian Museum, Calcutta, it appears that the shells before being used were bisected longitudinally, each half being hung as a pendant by one end from the cord encircling the neck, the whole forming a most uncomfortable-looking decoration, particularly as the custom is to wear them slung at the back of the neck.[1]

Sixty years ago chanks constituted the currency of the Naga tribes, but with the advent of the rupee, the consideration in which these shells was held largely disappeared, and now these quaint chank necklaces are seldom worn. Mr. Kemp saw them worn on only one or two occasions during the Abor expedition (1912).

At death these ornaments and all the other items of the deceased's dress, together with all his treasured weapons, are laid upon the grave.

Among the Abors the custom of wearing chank ornaments must be very rare, for Mr. Kemp, who most kindly gave attention to this subject, saw only a single instance—a Gam or headman of Komsing village, who was found wearing a necklace composed of round concave discs of shell.

The furthest point east to which I have been able to trace the use of chank discs is the banks of the Upper Mekong to the northward of Tali-fu in the Chinese Province of Yunnan. Here Prince Henri d'Orléans (" From Tonkin to India," p. 174, London, 1898) found the women of the wild Lissu tribe, a branch of the Lolo race, " often naked to the waist; they had a little hempen skirt and a Chinese cap decked with cowries and round white discs which are said to be brought from Thibet and looked to me as if cut out of large shells." In some villages they wore a heavy turban in place of the little white-disc'd cap.

The finest discs I have seen are prehistoric in age, having been taken from the very peculiar oblong sarcophagi, made of red pottery and raised on 6 or 8 stumpy legs, from the ancient graves at Perambair in the south of Chingleput District, near Madras. These discs, two in number, now on exhibit in the Madras Museum, are respectively about 2½ and 3 inches in diameter; in both there is a small central perforation. They appear to have been cut from the belly of large shells as the convexity is not great. The convex surface in each case is ornamented with geometrical patterns (different in each case) of much delicacy. One is illustrated on Pl. XXXIII. of the report for 1908–09 of the Director-General of Archæology.

The shape and size of these ornaments and the character of the incised patterns suggest that they have been used as boss ornaments for the back hair in the manner affected by native women of certain castes in South India. Until I had seen these ancient chank ornaments I had never heard of the chank shell being used for this purpose, but subsequently I have been told that the custom still survives in Travancore and that

[1] Similarly bisected chanks hung by a cord round the neck are also seen among the Chins of the Central and Northern sections of the Chin hills in Burma. My informant, Mr. W. Street, of the Burma Commission, states that the women alone wear this neck ornament; usually a single shell is used and apparently fresh supplies no longer come into the country as those now worn are heirlooms in the families of the wearers. It is probable that cessation of the supply synchronised with the discontinuance of chank shell currency among the Naga tribes living to the north of the Chin country.

when the wearers cannot afford gold these boss ornaments for the back hair may also be made from ivory, bone, horn and even coconut-shell. These are usually richly carved and frequently mounted in gold. The central hole in the chank disc would in such cases be used to secure the ornament to the hair.

Beads made from chank-shells do not seem to be used except to form bracelet and necklace amulets. I have seen no carefully worked and polished beads suitable for purely ornamental use. It is possible, however, that necklaces have been made from the pearls which are occasionally, but very rarely, found in the flesh (mantle) of the chank. Such pearls are not uncommon in the West Indian conch which produces them in sufficient frequency to constitute them regular items in the jewellery trade. These " pink pearls " as they are called, are usually made up into necklaces. The Indian chank is a much smaller shell, and although fished in far greater numbers than the West Indian shell, it is exceedingly rare for a pearl to be found. The colour of the few found varies from porcelain white to pale pink, and while it would be a matter of the greatest difficulty to obtain enough during many years' search to make a necklace, matching the colour and grading the size of the pearls to make the ornament a thing of beauty, is well-nigh an impossibility. I have three of these chank pearls in my possession; they are the only ones I have ever seen. The largest is a perfect sphere, $\frac{13}{32}$ inch in diameter, porcelain or opal white in colour, of lovely skin grained with a most peculiar mottling something after the fashion of the " watering " of watered silk. Another is slightly elongated in one axis ($\frac{5}{16}$ inch × $\frac{1}{4}$ inch), oval or elliptical in outline, of a very pale pink tint and possessing also the peculiar watered grain shown by its fellow. The third is salmon coloured, almost spherical, with a diameter of $\frac{11}{32}$ inch.

A few coat buttons are now made from chank-shells at Dacca—a recent departure on the part of one or two cutters who have made a feeble and ill-sustained attempt to open up new sources of demand. The main obstacle to the success of this new departure lies primarily in the lack of power-tools to cut up, drill and polish the material more cheaply than is possible so long as dependence is placed upon hand labour, however low be the wages paid. Granted even this change, great difficulties in the way of success exist in the lack of artistic versatility characterising the chank cutters' trade and the inability of the ordinary Indian manufacturer to appreciate the value of a judicious advertisement of his wares. He grudges to pay out money in advertisement and when he does so he usually brings about the loss he fears by lack of foresight in keeping up his stock of the advertised article or by the foolish as well as dishonest trick of sending an inferior article to that ordered and paid for by the customer who answers his advertisement.

With power machinery utilised by firms trading on sound and honest principles, there should be a very great field for the sale of chank buttons. There is nearly always a good demand for handsome buttons suitable for the decoration of ladies' jackets and coats and owing to the beautiful porcellaneous appearance of chank-shell when cut and engraved with some attractive or distinctive pattern, suitably designed buttons should meet with appreciation in the European and American dress trade. Rough cut buttons priced at what seems to the European ridiculously high rates are worse than useless, and beyond this the imagination of the Dacca manufacturer cannot soar —at present.

(*j*) FEEDING SPOUTS.

In the ordinary everyday life of the people of Southern India, the chank subserves several useful functions. Some of these have already been touched upon, but the most useful remains to be mentioned—that of small shells used as feeding spouts when weaning infants. The bazaars in every big Tamil town furnish these primitive utensils, made from undersized shells usually of the sub-fossil description obtained from the muddy lagoons near Jaffna in Ceylon.

The shells are prepared for market by breaking down parts of the inner portion of the terminal whorls just inside the mouth and by removing the central part of the columella. The canal-shaped canaliculum of the mouth is deepened and straightened to form a rough spout; the exterior surface of the shell is rubbed down and upon it is engraved a rude pattern, usually in the form of a spiral scroll with a few star-shaped emblems; last of all it receives a thin coating of fine lime or whitewash to hide imperfections and improve the colour (Pl. VI, Fig. 4). For the purpose intended it is quite effective, but how far the crevices of the interior, by offering obstacles to efficient cleansing, harbour and promote the rapid growth of bacteria and so lead directly to infantile diarrhœa, it is difficult to say. If the shell be boiled daily, a very simple precaution and easier to do in the case of a chank than in that of a glass bottle, there would be no danger, but I fear this is seldom thought of. In feeding baby monkeys just taken from their mother I have found this feeding shell most useful; the sight of the little creature hanging on with both fore-paws to the shell, half choking in its eagerness to swallow the milk and all the time trying to locate every noise and movement in the room with its great nervous eyes is one of the quaintest pictures imaginable.

(*k*) CURRENCY.

That the chank once served a savage people as a form of currency is little known, but so it was in the Naga country of Assam until less than 50 years ago. Major-General John Butler, who commanded an early expedition into the Naga hills, tells (*loc. cit.*, p. 157) that he found the Nagas of many villages using chank-shells as currency with a fixed and thoroughly well-determined exchange value relative to the price of all articles of trade. Slaves and cattle in particular were always valued in chank-shells. Thus while a male slave was worth one cow and three chank-shells, a female slave—

much more valuable, the suffragettes will learn with pleasure, than a mere man—was worth as much as three cows and four or five chank-shells. Now a cow was valued at ten chank-shells, a pig at two shells, a goat was the same rate, and a fowl at one packet of salt. As a chank-shell was considered worth one rupee, a short calculation will show that a male slave was worth Rs. 13, and a female slave Rs. 34, or 34 shells. The ransoms of villages captured during raids in these good old days were largely paid in chank-shells, beads, cows, pigs and other portable wealth. Chank-shells and beads were the chief items of currency, but even in Butler's time the inevitable invasion of the rupee was already successful in the valleys most accessible to low-country traders. At the village of Hosang-hajoo the chief remarked to Major Butler, with a show of considerable pride, "since we became British subjects, we have paid revenue in coin and with it we can procure anything we require; we therefore no longer want shells and beads."

I see no reason to believe that chank currency ever extended beyond the hill peoples of Assam and possibly some of the adjoining hill tracts. On some coins issued by the ancient Pandiyan and Chalukyan dynasties of southern India a chank-shell appears as the principal symbol (Thurston, I, 328); this might be held as evidence of a preceding currency consisting of the actual object so represented, whereof the memory was perpetuated in pictorial form upon one face of the coins and tokens which came to take its place as more convenient units of exchange. But there is much more reason to believe that the chank was represented on such coins for a similar reason to that which actuates the present-day States of Travancore and Cochin to adopt a similar symbol on their current coins. In these two States, the homes of southern Hindu orthodoxy, the chank-shell symbolises the religious belief of the ruling race and is their emblem as the rose stands for England and the thistle for Scotland. Both these States utilised it as a distinctive symbol on their earliest issues of local postage stamps in place of and to the exclusion of the sovereign's head—the customary pivot of design in European stamps.

Both the States of Travancore and Cochin also employ the chank in their recently designed armorial bearings. In the case of Travancore, the arms described in heraldic terms consist of :—Argent, on a fesse azure, three reversed (sinistral) chank-shells or; Crest—a sea-horse proper. Motto—*Dharmosmat Kuladevatam*. In Cochin the shield bears more numerous devices; in addition to a left-handed chank, a palanquin, a brass lamp and an umbrella are depicted, with elephant supporters as in the case of Travancore. In all cases where these States use the chank symbol, it is necessary to note that it should occur in the abnormal sinistral or reversed form, this being the Royal and Sacred Chank—the Chank of Vishnu.

When the Maharaja of Travancore performs *tulabharam*, a coronation ceremony wherein he weighs himself in scales against gold, special gold coins are struck called tulabhāra kāsu (*cf.* our Maundy money). On one side a figure of a chank-shell appears, on the other the legend "Sri Padmanābha" in Malayalam characters. After the ceremony these coins are distributed among the Brahmans who have assembled from all parts of the country.

(*l*) CHANK LIME.

A minor use to which chank-shells are put in the coastal districts where they occur, and also in those localities in Bengal where bangle factories exist, is to calcine these in kilns. The lime so produced is esteemed the best quality obtainable in India, fully equal to, if not better than, that obtained by burning pearl oyster shells. The auspicious nature of the shell adds further value to the product, and when a temple or shrine or specially fine newly-built house has to be whitewashed, chank lime is greatly sought after for this purpose in the Tamil districts. I have even received petitions praying that permission be granted for the collection of chanks for this purpose.

At the present day the fact that almost all the produce of the South Indian chank fisheries is exported to Bengal, makes it very difficult to obtain chank lime—the shells are too valuable to calcine. That it was not so in former times, in some cases at least, is to be seen if we inspect the walls of the old temples at Korkai, the seat of the Tinnevelly chank fishery 800 to 2,000 years ago. The mortar still contains many recognisable fragments of chank-shells.

(*m*) IN MEDICINE.

Apart from the uses to which chank rings and bracelets are put as amulets against certain ailments, the shell itself in several ways is used medicinally. Except in cases which have come under my personal notice, it is somewhat difficult to ascertain the exact nature of the diseases for which native practitioners employ this specific; custom appears to vary with different districts and even with different "doctors" living in the same town.

Of some there is no doubt. The belief is general throughout Tamil districts and Malabar that water which has been in contact with an article formed from a chaṇk-shell is a charm against and a remedy for blotches, pimples and other skin troubles on the face and body. A chank ring worn on a finger is an easy way of applying the remedy, as water applied to the face or body by the hand must necessarily have been in contact with chank substance and so able to transmit the virtue thereof. This remedy is believed to act still more beneficially if the ring be rubbed upon the affected parts. In South Arcot, Tanjore, Coimbatore, Salem and Trichinopoly, certain skin diseases, eruptions, warts and even hæmorrhoids are believed to yield to this treatment. In Coimbatore native doctors prescribe a paste made by mixing chank powder in water or by rubbing it up with human milk for use as a salve in the case of eruptions (sties) on the eyelids. Chank ointments (basmams) are also employed in the same district to cure inflammation of the eye, the growth of bad flesh (granulation) on the interior surface of the eyelids and also for piles and leprosy.

Chank-shell in the form of powder is also stated to be taken internally in South Arcot, Salem, Madura and Tinnevelly, either in water or mixed with ghee, as a specific for skin eruptions, asthma, coughs, and also to cool the system. In Salem and also in Ceylon it is used as a remedy for consumption. Both in Tanjore and Salem mixed with milk or water it is also employed as a salve or lotion applied to pimples and boils. In Malabar and South Canara, I am told, it is used in the case of rickets (*grahani*), chank ring powder ground in water being rubbed on the breast. At Tanur a street quack told me he used chank-shell powder internally as a remedy in cases of *varchcha* (gonorrhœa, I believe).

Among the Tuticorin Parawas a mixture of camphor and chank powder is commonly used to relieve soreness of the eyes. A small piece of camphor is partially burned and then ground down in a small quantity of human milk upon a flat stone by means of a small well-cleaned chank-shell ; a small amount of powder from the shell is thus incorporated with this peculiar ointment ; sometimes the white of an egg is substituted for human milk. The ointment thus made is applied round the eyelids ; it is reputed to effect a sure and speedy cure.

Pounded chank-shell is also given internally by native practitioners in Trichinopoly, Salem and Coimbatore to those who suffer from an acute form of dyspepsia called *kunman*. It is administered after each meal—a treatment perfectly rational as the carbonate of lime of which the shell is composed is well adapted to counteract hyperacidity of the gastric fluids.

In Gujarat and Kathiawar chank powder is prescribed as a specific in the following diseases :—Jaundice, phthisis, coughs, shooting pain in the side, general debility and, very commonly, in affections of the eyes.

With regard to the practice of prescribing it in the case of asthma, cough and consumption, a medical friend points out that while of no value in asthma, this treatment has reason for its employment in phthisical cases—the introduction of quantities of lime into the system facilitating the deposit of lime salts around tubercular centres, encapsulating them and rendering them innocuous.

In rickets the use of lime taken internally is also indicated emphatically, the disease being characterised by an insufficient deposit of lime in the bones. He also points out that in the case of hæmorrhoids, the use of lime administered internally may assist a cure by increasing the coagulative property of the patient's blood.

It appears therefore that the employment of chank-shell powder by native practitioners is not without reason in regard to certain diseases, and while it may be objected that a non-organic form of carbonate of lime should prove equally beneficial, it has to be remembered that the carbonate of lime of shells is laid down within a delicate framework of animal membrane, and this minutely divided form may possibly render it more easy of assimilation in the body and therefore more efficacious. The religious associations surrounding the chank have also their value in inspiring the confidence of patients in the value of this medicine, faith that may help largely towards a cure.

The wearing of chank rings, the rubbing of the affected parts with them and the laving of them with water which has been in contact with these rings, are forms of treatment on a different footing. They are to be considered purely as charms, without direct therapeutic value. They bear the same relation to the internal employment of powdered shell as does the quack exploitation of electricity by means of belts and bands containing discs of metal to the legitimate use of current electricity in the hands of qualified medical practitioners. If the former have any value it is by reason of faith alone.

The egg-capsule of the chank is employed by the chank and pearl divers of Tuticorin to relieve headache. They grind up a portion of the egg-capsule (sanku-pu or "chank-flower") in gingelly-oil, together with pepper and coriander seed, and apply the paste to the forehead and temples.

Finally, according to Risley (II, p. 223) the shell-workers of Dacca are accustomed to extract the dried remnant of the visceral coil (called *pitta*) from the shells they receive and to sell this to native physicians as a medicine for spleen enlargement. He also states that the dust produced in sawing the shells is employed to prevent the pitting of small-pox and as an ingredient of a valuable white paint.

(*n*) FOOD.

During the run home from the chank beds, the divers are accustomed to extract the foot and anterior part of the body of the chank from the shells they have collected. The work is roughly performed by means of a pointed iron rod and all the apical mass, comprising the hepatic and reproductive glands, remains within the shell. What is extracted consists almost entirely of tough muscular tissue carrying the adherent horny operculum at one end. These fragments are collected in the little palmyra-leaf baskets used for bailing water out of the canoe. The flesh, called *chanku-chathai*, is carried home and there prepared for family use. The preparation consists of separating the operculum, boiling the flesh for a short time and then cutting the foot and head region transversely into thin slices. These are dried in the sun; when required for use they are fried in oil and eaten with rice and curry stuffs. On one occasion I essayed to try this much-esteemed food, but my taste was not sufficiently cultivated; the fried slices tasted or rather smelled like frizzled shoe-leather and were altogether too tough for my teeth.

(*o*) INCENSE STICKS.

The horny operculum is also put to use. It is dried, reduced to powder, and then employed, after soaking in water, as an adhesive matrix to bind together the powdered sandal-wood and other sweet-smelling incense material used in coating the incense sticks burned before shrines, or used in native shops. In Tamil these sticks go by the names of uthupaththi or sāmbirānik-kuchchi ; the best quality sells at the rate of 1 or 2 for 3 pies, while inferior sorts retail at from ½ to 1 pie each. The operculum itself is called nāganam or nāvanam ; the usual rate is 2 annas per palam (=8 tolas or just over 3 oz.).

(*p*) ASSEMBLY CALLS, ETC.

A call on a chank-shell is frequently employed upon native-owned plantations in South India and Ceylon to summon the workpeople to their duties : there can be no doubt that these long drawn out and penetrating booming calls are particularly well adapted to this purpose.

In the Laccadive Islands all the inhabitants are required under penalty to attend the call of the chank, sounded in cases of emergency and public requirement. Among these are counted the beaching of boats and the inauguration of rat hunts.

To conclude this account of the miscellaneous uses to which the chank is put and of which the foregoing summary has by no means exhausted the list, the following instance of the ingenuity of the Indian countryman may not be amiss. For it I am indebted to Mr. C. A. Innes, I.C.S. Apropos of a flight of winged termites, he told me that once when travelling in the Madura district, he chanced upon a low caste man engaged upon some mysterious work on a large termite anthill : the man had a chank-shell in his hand. When asked what he was doing, he replied, " I am catching white ants to eat," and gave a blast upon the chank at one of the major openings into the hill. Hardly had he finished ere crowds of ants sallied forth from other openings, and these the man scooped up in handfuls and ate without any preparation.

IV.

THE USE OF CHANK BANGLES.

(1) IN NORTHERN INDIA.

(2) IN THE MADRAS PRESIDENCY.

(1) *In Northern India.*—Although evidence is strong in favour of the belief that the custom of wearing chank bracelets was in old times prevalent throughout the length and breadth of India, more especially in the Tamil country, in the Deccan, in Kathiawar, Gujarat, and Bengal, at the present day only in Bengal, the adjacent hill regions to the west, north, and east and in a few Tamil-speaking districts in the extreme south of India, does the custom continue to be widely observed and of notable social importance.

In Bengal and wherever in the adjoining Provinces of Assam, Behar and Orissa there are colonies of the Bengali race, every married woman of all castes which are thoroughly Hinduised is bound to possess a pair of chank bangles lacquered in vermilion as one of the visible tokens of her married state; the red sankha, or shakha as it is called in Dacca, is indeed as necessary of assumption during the marriage ceremonies as is the performance of that other Hindu custom of smearing a streak of vermilion on the forehead or down the parting of the bride's hair or as the wedding ring of English women. Garcia da Orta's curious statement quoted on page 73 is to be explained in the light of this custom; his informants doubtless meant to convey no more than that among the better classes an essential part of the marriage ceremony consisted in placing chank bracelets on the arms of the bride. The women of castes holding good social status appear, however, to have no great liking for the custom, particularly if their husbands be well-to-do, and I was informed that they frequently lay them aside temporarily in favour either of more handsomely carved ones or replace them when means permit by gold and jewelled ones. Chank bangles are occasionally ornamented with gold and set with jewels; the price of these may reach several hundreds of rupees. The great majority of married women, however, wear them permanently, never removing them so long as their husbands are alive. Occasionally some of the modern sankha (marriage) bangles are made in two sections secured together after the bangle is placed on the wrist by means of tiny bamboo pins as it is otherwise impossible to pass one of the right size over the hand without great difficulty and the infliction of acute pain.

In spite of the rapid spread of a desire for bracelets of more showy appearance, there are very large numbers of prosperous Hindu households, especially in the country districts, where the womenfolk remain attached to the old and less ostentatious custom of wearing chank bangles solely as ornaments. Among these conservative folk a large demand exists for the handsome products of the sankhari workshops. The ornamental bangles made to meet these requirements are of two kinds called respectively *bàla* and *chùri*. The former are broad bangles worn one on each wrist. The *chùri* on the con-

TEXT-FIGURE 1.

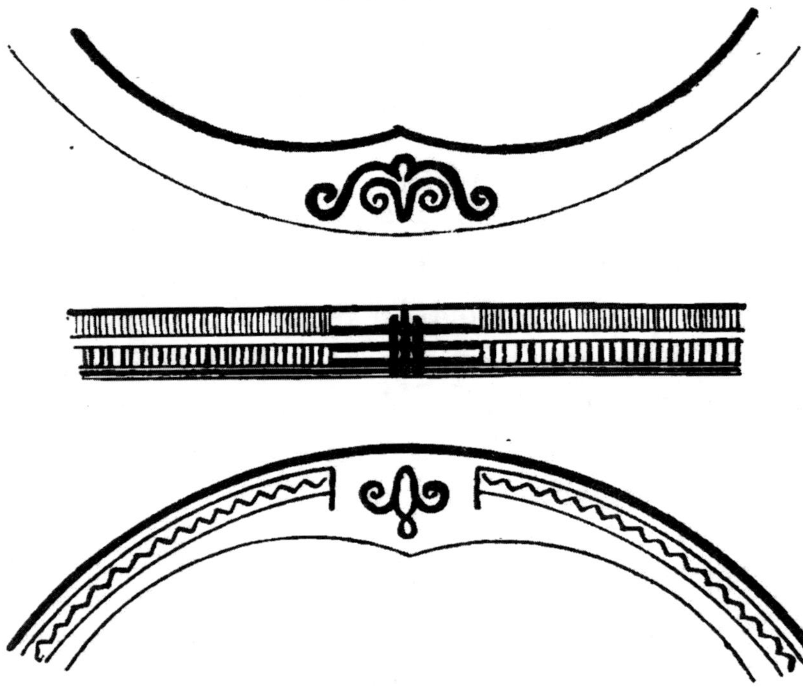

Edge and side views of a Bengal marriage bangle to show ornamentation in yellow upon a red-lacquered ground. From Pabna, Bengal. × 2.

trary is always quite narrow, generally $\frac{1}{6}$ to $\frac{1}{5}$ inch in width, and usually of conventional scroll design, worn in a set of three on each wrist.

The use of these ornamental bangles (*bàla* and *chùri*) and also of the red marriage bangle is limited almost entirely to the thoroughly Hinduised sections of the Bengali people, together with the Hindu communities settled in Assam, Behar and Orissa. Baishnab women, however, do not wear these bangles according to the Collector of Birbhum. Information received from a Muhammadan source indicates that women of the lower classes of this community in Dacca, Darjeeling and Assam occasionally wear chank bangles as wrist ornaments.

As elsewhere in India, it is the invariable custom in Bengal in orthodox Hindu households for widows to discard all their jewellery on the death of their husbands. In the case of chank and glass bangles, it is usual for the widow to break and throw them away on the first occasion when she bathes after her husband's death. They never resume the use of similar bangles except in the very rare cases where re-marriage is permitted to widows. Tavernier says [1] "when a man dies, all his relatives and friends should come to the interment and when they place the body in the ground they take off all the bracelets which are on their arms and legs and bury them with the defunct." This burial of the widow's bangles with the dead may still be continued by some castes, but as earth-burial is now rapidly being displaced by cremation as orthodox Hinduism secures a firmer hold on the people, this custom must tend to die out. Generally in Bengal the Hindu women wear sankhas as visible tokens of the possession of living husbands. The Hindu Shastras are said to enjoin their use as it is believed that this contributes to the prosperity and longevity of their husbands.

Surti, Tuticorin and Rameswaram chanks are necessary in the manufacture of both *bàla* and *chùri* bangles as these require to be made from the finest quality of shells —those possessing a pure white porcellaneous appearance and a dense well-conditioned substance susceptible of high polish.

Among Bengal castes of inferior social status, particularly those whose physical characteristics bespeak Dravidian descent and whose customs are not yet thoroughly Hinduised the use of chank bangles made up into massive gauntlets composed of numerous separate bangles is very prevalent. Prominent among these are the widely spread Kochh tribe in their two principal sub-divisions of Rajbansi and Paliya. It is largely to supply the women of this tribe with their characteristic ornaments that the chank bangle workshops in Dinajpur and Rangpur exist, as in these districts the tribe has its chief settlement with an approximate total of one million individuals. Kuch Behar and Jalpaiguri account for another half million, while considerable numbers are found also in Purnia, Maldah, the Darjeeling Terai, Bogra, Murshidabad, Nadiya and Dacca. The Rajbansi and Paliya gauntlets are composed usually of ten separate bangles. As the wearers belong largely to the labouring and agricultural classes the bangles forming these gauntlets are broad and thick, frequently without any ornament whatever; where decoration is attempted, it consists of simple line patterns made of shallow groovings which impair very little the strength of the bangle and yet are very effective and elegant (Text-figure 2). Neither are they usually polished, hence dead shells from Jaffna are largely employed in this manufacture, although inferior shells of the better qualities from the Indian side are also extensively made use of.

The Muchi is another important Bengal caste where the wearing of numerous chank bangles is a distinctive custom among the women. This is a leather-dressing and cobbler caste, socially a shade higher than the allied Chamārs from whom the Muchis appear to be an offshoot. One of the obvious distinctions between the women of these castes lies in the character of the bracelets worn. Thus while the female Chamār prides herself on huge bracelets of bell metal adorning her arms, the Muchi woman always substitutes chank bangles. The Muchis, like the Paraiyar of the South, are largely

[1] *Loc. cit.*, Vol. II, p. 285.

the caste drummers of the province and as they are fond of the violin and the pipe are usually employed as musicians at Hindu weddings.

In Western Bengal and in Behar the Santāls take the place occupied by the Rajbansis and Paliyas in North-Eastern and Eastern Bengal as the chief chank bangle wearing tribe. Many of their women follow the same habit of disposing of a number of chank bangles, three to five usually, as a massive cuff-like gauntlet or compound bracelet. These people being generally poor, the quality employed for these compound bracelets is inferior and red and yellow lac are freely used upon them to enhance their appearance and to disguise imperfections. Many indeed are too poor to afford these ornaments and others belong to families which do not observe the custom; in Birbhum which

TEXT-FIGURE 2.

Gauntlet pattern of compound bracelet worn by Paliya women, Bengal.

may be taken as a characteristic Santāl district, it is estimated that about half the female Santāl population follow this custom. Sometimes Santāl girls wear them from an early age but generally they are assumed at marriage. It has no religious significance and marriage may be performed without the putting on of these bangles which are worn more for ornament and because of custom than for any more serious reason. Like the Hindus, Santāl women break and throw away their bangles on the occasion of widowhood, re-assuming others, if they wish, if they remarry. Dead shells are often employed by the cutters for Santāl bangles.

Risley states (II, p. 225) that the Santāls in point of physical characteristics may be regarded as typical examples of the pure Dravidian stock and in view of the similar origin attributed to the Kochh tribe which includes both the Rajbansi and the Paliya, this becomes a matter of great significance as well as of much difficulty, for whereas the Kochh people are professed Hindus, the Santāls hold the animistic beliefs characteristic of Non-Hinduised Dravidians. However Oldham, as quoted by Risley (I, p. 492), states that " the adhesion of the Kochh tribe to Hinduism is comparatively recent as shown by their own customs as regards burial, food and marriage."

The section of the Kurmi caste found in Chota Nagpore and Orissa also wear chank bangles. In view of what has been said above in regard to the Dravidian origin of the Kochhs and Santāls, it is of importance to find that Risley (I, p. 530) considers this territorial section of the caste as undoubtedly Dravidian, as shown by their physical characteristics, religious beliefs and social customs. In appearance, he says that in Munbhum and the north of Orissa, it is difficult to distinguish a Kurmi from a Bhumij or a Santāl. In their religion the animistic beliefs characteristic of the Dravidian races are overlaid by the thinnest veneer of conventional Hinduism, and the vague shapes of ghosts and demons who haunt the jungles and the rocks are the real powers to whom the Kurmi looks for the ordering of his moral and physical welfare.

Alike with the Santāls the internal structure of that branch of the Kurmi caste living in Chota Nagpur and Orissa is founded upon a distinct and well-defined totemism in which a large proportion of the totems are still capable of being identified. Risley (II, appendix, p. 88) enumerates 60 totemistic sections or septs in this caste, among which is one termed Sankhawār whose members are prohibited from wearing chank shell ornaments. Among the Santāls, the place of this sept is taken by one called Sankh, wherein all individuals are forbidden, under pain of caste punishment, the use of the chank shell in any form ; they may neither cut, burn, nor use the shell, nor may the women of this sept use it in personal adornment (I, p. xliii).

The prevalence of the use of chank bangles among these Dravidian races, the present animistic beliefs of the Santāls and Chota Nagpur Kurmis, and the comparatively recent renunciation of the same cult by the great Kochh tribe, taken in conjunction with other facts and especially with the widely spread archæological finds detailed elsewhere in these pages, point to the use of chank bangles as having had a purely Dravidian origin and as having been a custom prevalent and solidly established among at least certain sections of the race throughout India anterior to the advent of the Aryan invaders and the rise of the Brahmanic faith. The cult of the chank would therefore appear to be one adopted (and modified) by the Brahmans from the religious belief which they found indigenous to India.

Finally, in the hill tracts of Chittagong, we find the women of the Maghs, a race of Indo-Mongolian extraction and Buddhists by religion, using very broad unornamented sections of chank shells as bracelets in similar manner as we shall next see is the habit in Thibet and Bhutan, inhabited by other Mongolian races. To supply the needs of the Maghs, bangle cutters are established in Chittagong; these work-people are chiefly Muhammadans and the work they do is of the roughest and crudest description in conformity with the undeveloped artistic taste of their customers who appear to wear these bracelets rather as amulets than as ornaments. Broad arm ornaments of similar simple form are used by the Papuans and by the wild inhabitants of several groups of the Melanesian islands; sometimes round the wrist, sometimes on the upper arm above the elbow. I do not know, however, whether the shell employed in these instances be Turbinella or not. Among these island tribes it is the men who wear these ornaments.

Outside of Bengal and Assam the only considerable demand for chank bracelets comes from Thibet and Bhutan. The trade is one of long standing, for Tavernier, in 1666, found Bhutanese merchants taking home from Pabna and Dacca bracelets sawn from "sea-shells as large as an egg." He also states that 2,000 men were occupied in these two places in making tortoise-shell and sea-shell bracelets and "all that is produced by them is exported [1] to the kingdoms of Bhutan, Assam, Siam and other countries to the north and east of the territories of the great Moghul" (*loc. cit.*, p. 267).

Chank bangles appear to be worn very generally throughout Thibet, from Ladakh in the west to the Kham country in the east. Neve records [2] seeing the poorer women in Kashmiri Thibet wearing broad shell-bangles in shape like a cuff on both wrists, while on the march of the British expedition to Lhassa in 1904 they were noted as in frequent use by Thibetan women. This ornament is assumed early in life while the hand is still small and pliable; after a few years it becomes impossible to remove it without breakage which these women will suffer only in the last resort, as it cannot be replaced except by one of large diameter which will fit more loosely on the arm than they like. A medical officer with the Thibet mission has informed me that in one instance a Thibetan woman was brought to him for the treatment of a festering wound on the wrist. On examination the cause of the trouble was found to be the presence of a chank bangle so small that the wrist had been wounded and circulation impeded; gangrene was imminent and although the woman was loth to part with her bangle it had to be filed off to save the hand.

The export of round and square discs of chank shell to the Buddhist countries of the north appears to be much less than in Tavernier's time, as it is now comparatively insignificant. Among the Nāgas, the discs are employed to ornament the men's hair-bedecked helmets, and Prince Henri d'Orléans [3] found the women of the wild Lissus,

[1] Evidently a *lapsus calami* as the custom of wearing chank bangles was even more prevalent in Tavernier's day among Bengali women than it is to-day, *vide* Orta, *loc. cit.*

[2] "Beyond the Pir Panjal," London, 1912.

[3] "From Tonkin to India," English Translation, London, 1898.

a section of the Lolo tribe, mountaineers living in the upper valley of the Mekong in Yunnan, employing chank shell discs to ornament their Chinese caps. It may be that these Lissus and cognate tribes represent those chank jewel wearers whom Tavernier refers to as belonging to the kingdom of Siam. In this latter country at the present day I know of no utilisation of chanks in personal adornment.

The chank is one of the eight lucky signs recognised by Buddhists of the Northern cult and as such is constantly reproduced in Buddhist ornamentation in Thibet and Bhutan.[1] It may therefore be inferred that the use of it in personal adornment has a like reason; whether in the form of a bangle, a cap or a hair ornament, a necklace or a breast disc, it is employed as a talisman to ensure good fortune, and possibly even as an amulet against the evil eye, as is the chank shell placed on the forehead of draft bulls in Southern India.

(2) *The Tribes and Castes which wear Chank Bangles in the South of India.*

In the Madras Presidency and the associated native States, the castes whose women systematically wear chank bangles are few, and if we except the wandering tribes of the Lambadis (or Brinjaris), Koravars and Kurivikkarans, the custom appears confined to a sub-division of each caste or tribe. Whether it had a totemistic origin and significance as it still has among non-Hinduised tribes in Bengal, Behar and Chota Nagpur is not at present clear. If it had, the original tribal sept, usually exogamous, has become changed to a caste sub-division, invariably endogamous. And whereas among the septs of those animistic tribes in Northern India which are named after the chank this shell is taboo with them, it forms the characteristic ornament of the women of the caste sub-divisions named after it, in Southern India.

Only in the Kongu country, which coincides roughly with the present inland districts of Coimbatore and Salem, does the custom continue to flourish at all strongly. Coimbatore is the great centre of the custom, for there the numbers of chank-bangle wearers greatly exceed those found in any other district. The Collector reports eleven castes and sub-divisions as following this custom, viz. :—

(1) Pala Vellalas.
(2) Puluvans (so-called Puluva Vellalas).
(3) Konga and Golla Idaiyans.
(4) Konga Shanans.
(5) Konga Vannans.
(6) Thotti Chukkiliyans.
(7) Sangu, Konga, Sangudu or Sanguvalai Paraiyans.
(8) Thottiya Naiks.
(9) Okkilians (not universal).
(10) Kurumbars.
(11) Lambadis in parts of Kollegal and Gobichettipalaiyam divisions.

[1] J. Claude White, "Sikhim and Bhutan," p. 46. London, 1909.

The custom is associated particularly with those caste sub-divisions whose territorial cognomen indicates a long settled residence in the Kongu country (Coimbatore and Salem). The Konga sub-divisions of the Idaiyar, Paraiyar, Vannar and Shanar castes have this custom in common and as several other castes in Coimbatore also adhere to it, we may infer that at one time the custom was general in the Kongu country among at least the generality of the lower castes.

Another caste sub-division where the women wear chank bangles is that of the Sangukatti Idaiyans. Among them the marriage ceremony requires, as in Bengal, the placing of a chank bangle on one of the bride's wrists.

Among Coimbatore castes the chank bangle is worn always upon the left wrist, usually singly but occasionally a pair in certain cases, *e.g.*, among the Konga Paraiyans.

The wearing of these bangles is considered as a symbol of the permanence of the marriage tie, a belief probably derived from the custom of breaking the bangle after the death of the husband. The Collector of Coimbatore states that a widow discards her bangle one month after her husband's death. He adds that if a woman accidentally breaks her bangle, she thinks it unlucky and regards it as an omen that her husband will chance on some evil; when the husband is sick the wife prays that it may be her good fortune to wear the bangle during her whole life. A woman considers it improper to appear before her husband or in public without the bangle. The wearing of this ornament appears to be followed in Coimbatore largely because it is an ancient custom, with no further significance beyond what is implied above. It is not now connected with belief in the evil-eye though it is said to have had this significance in former times. The general belief in the efficacy of the chank as a specific against skin diseases may however be counted as one of the obscure reasons for its continued usage.

The practice is more general among low castes. The Collectors of Madura and Trichinopoly both inform me that among Paraiyans, Chukkiliyans (leather workers, etc.), Oddans, Koravas and the Naick sections known as Kavaraja and Thottiya Kambalathans, together with the wandering tribe of Lambadis, the custom of wearing chank bangles is found to prevail here and there in both districts. There appears to be no general observance of the custom—in some villages and taluks none among the women of the castes named wears chank bangles; elsewhere, as in the Nāmakkal Taluk (Trichinopoly District), a definite section of the Paraiyan caste called Sengudimi Paraiyans adopts this ornament as a distinguishing sept distinction, while in other parts of the country, the women of these various low castes wear it chiefly if not entirely for its ornamental value. The custom appears to be dying out, as witness the vagueness of the people who still adhere to its observance as to the reason for so doing, its partial and sporadic geographical distribution in the districts where it lingers, and the comparatively small numbers who adhere to it. As a typical instance of the irregular distribution of the custom, the report of the Collector of Trichinopoly states that in the Musiri and Kārūr Taluks, no people wear chank-bangles; in Nāmakkal Taluk only the Paraiyan sept call Sengudimi Paraiyans wear them; in Udaiyārpālaiyam Taluk the habit is confined to Koravans and Lambadis; in Trichinopoly and Perambalūr Taluks to Chukkiliyans and Paraiyans, while in Kulittalai Taluk besides the two castes just named, the Oddans, Koravans and Thottia Naickers are given as castes following the custom—it is to be noted that all are amongst the lowest of castes, constituting what may be termed the inferior labouring population. The bangles employed are manufactured in Kilakarai and pass to Trichinopoly by the intermediary of traders in Madura. The price in Trichinopoly town is from Rs. 3 to 4 per 100 bangles, all very roughly made, with little or no ornamentation.

In Tanjore and Salem the Paraiyans and Chukkiliyans use chank-bangles in certain villages and these Salem Pariayans are said to belong to the Konga division as in Coimbatore. In both districts the Lambadis and Koravas have the same custom, and the Collector of Tanjore adds that the women of the Uppu Koravar, Panni Koravar, and Vari Koravar sub-divisions, together with the Oddar and Domba castes, all agree in following the habit. He states that the Koravas put on the bangles during the marriage ceremonies.

In Salem the Malayali women of the Chitteri Hills, Uttangarai Taluk, also use chank-bangles.

Hawkers called Dasam Chettis, who bring their wares from Rāmēswaram and Kilakarai, attend village fairs and temple festivals with these bangles in Salem and Coimbatore, charging from 4 to 12 annas a pair. In Coimbatore well-to-do Puluva Vellalans not infrequently wear bangles of superior quality costing even Rs. 3 to 5 per pair; these probably are brought from Calcutta, as no expensive patterns are made at Kilakarai. In Tanjore about the same prices prevail, but here the most expensive, said to come from Calcutta, are said to cost one rupee per pair; common qualities as usual come from the Rāmnād coast.

In the Nilgiri hills, especially in Ootacamund, Konga Paraiyan women who have come from Coimbatore are often to be met with wearing chank-bangles. Their subdivision is considered one of superior standing and the people belonging to it will not act as sweepers. The bangle is always worn on the left wrist; frequently two are worn, always plain and massive, and about $\frac{3}{8}$ inch in width, exactly similar indeed to those worn by Chanku (Puluva ?) Vellalas.

The women of the Kota hill-tribe in the Nilgiri hills have an allied custom, but instead of a massive bangle cut from the entire shell, they wear around the left wrist a bracelet of roughly-made chank beads strung on a thread. When chank beads are not obtainable they wear a string of white glass beads as near the colour and shape of the usual chank beads as they can obtain. In answer to my questions, the elders of a Kota village situated close to Kotagiri informed me that all married women must possess and wear one of these bracelets on the left wrist together with two massive copper bangles on the right wrist during their husband's life. They are assumed, however, before marriage, and the putting on of the chank bracelet is not a part of the marriage ceremonies. On the death of the husband the widow discards this with her other ornaments, but is permitted to resume them after a decent interval of mourning—three months according to my informant. It is to be noted that the wife's ornaments are not broken or destroyed at the husband's death as is the custom among the chank-wearing Hinduised plains-people. At the woman's own death they are put to burn with her body on the funeral pyre. The Kotas can adduce no special reason for the wearing of these bracelets, except that their god Bhagawani long ago ordered that their women should do so.

From the foregoing it is seen that chank-bangle wearing is confined to the Tamil districts in the south of the Madras Presidency. It is unknown in the central and northern sections—the Madras Deccan and the coastal Telugu districts—except in respect of the wandering Lambadis; the Collector of Kurnul informs me that chank-bangles for sale to the local representatives of this tribe are occasionally brought from the Raichur side (Hyderabad State), a significant fact as the Raichur Doab is one of the localities where Mr. Bruce-Foote found numerous fragments of chank factory waste, indicative of the former existence of a bangle-making industry in the vicinity of his discoveries. Where these modern Raichur bangles come from I do not know, but I should expect them to be of Bengal manufacture.

(1) The Antiquity of the Chank-Bangle Industry.

(*a*) in the Tinnevelly district.

Reference to ancient Tamil classics furnishes evidence scanty but conclusive of the existence of an important chank-cutting industry in the ancient Pandyan kingdom in the early centuries of the Christian era. Similar evidence is also extant of a widespread use of carved and ornamented chank bangles in former days by the women of the Pandyan country which may be considered as roughly co-extensive with the modern districts of Tinnevelly, Madura, and Rāmnād, forming the eastern section of the extreme south of the Madras Presidency.

Among the more important references which prove the ancient importance of this industry on the Indian shore of the Gulf of Mannar, is one contained in the "*Maduraikkanchi*," a Tamil poem which incidentally describes the ancient city of Korkai, once the sub-capital of the Pandyan kingdom and the great emporium familiar to Greek and Egyptian sailors and traders and described by the geographers of the 1st and 2nd centuries A.D. under the name of Kolkhoi. From the purity of the Tamil employed in this poem and the similarity of the names of the towns, ports and goods mentioned incidentally with those employed by Ptolemy and the author of the "Periplus of the Erythræan Sea," we may date it as approximately contemporaneous with the writings of these authors and certainly not later than the 2nd or 3rd century A.D.

In one passage (LL. 140-144) the Parawas are described as men who dived for pearl oysters and for chank shells and knew charms to keep sharks away from that part of the sea where diving was being carried on. Another passage depicts the city of Korkai, then a seaport at the mouth of the Tambraparni, as the chief town in the country of the Parawas and the seat of the pearl fishery, with a population consisting chiefly of pearl-divers and chank-cutters. The great epic, the *Silappathikkarram*, or "Lay of the Anklet," written about the same period by a Jain poet, gives further information about Korkai, from which we gather that on account of the great value of the revenue derived from the pearl fishery, this city was a sub-capital of the Pandyan realm and the usual residence of the heir-apparent, boasting great magnificence and adorned with temples and palaces befitting its wealth and importance.

Another valuable reference to the chank trade is contained in two Tamil stanzas which chronicle a passage at arms between a Brahman and Nakkirar, the celebrated poet-president of the Madura Sangam in the reign of the Pandyan king Nedunj Cheliyan II, who flourished probably about the beginning of the 2nd century A.D.

The Brahman, named Dharmi, presented to the Sangam a poem purporting to be composed with the aid of Siva. Nakkirar, the President, in spite of its alleged divine origin criticised the poem mercilessly, and rejected it as unworthy of literary recognition. The Brahman took revenge by presenting another poem also purporting to be inspired by Siva; in it he held the President up to ridicule on account of his caste trade in pungent lines which may be translated literally as follows :—

"Is Kiran fit to criticise my poem? Spreading his knees wide, his joints loosened (by the labour) does he not saw chanks into sections, his ghee-smeared saw murmuring the while kir—kir?"

Besides the insult intended to be given, the verse contains a play on the President's name and the sound given out during the sawing of chank shells.

The reply of Nakkirar was "Chank-cutting is indeed the calling of my caste; of that I am not ashamed. But of what caste is Sankara? (one of the many names of Siva). We earn our livelihood by cutting chanks; we do not live by begging as he did"—an allusion to the fable popularised by the Brahmans wherein Siva is represented as a mendicant seeking alms with a skull in his hand as begging bowl.

Dharmi's description of a chank-cutter's trade is wonderfully vivid in the original Tamil; in a dozen words he paints a realistic word-picture of a cutter's workshop—the men seated on the ground with the knees widely spread and depressed outwards almost to the ground to give free play to the great crescentic two-handled saw monotonously droning a single note as it cuts its way laboriously through the hard substance of the shell.

Tradition has it that Nakkirar, the chank-cutter President of the Sangam, was a Parawa by caste. It would be most appropriate if this be correct as we have already seen that at the beginning of the Christian era chank-fishing and chank-cutting were among the important trades carried on in Korkai, the chief settlement of the Parawas in early days.

No Parawas to-day are engaged in chank-cutting although they still largely monopolise the shore industries of Tinnevelly where they continue as from time immemorial to provide the contingent of divers required for the exploitation of both the pearl- and the chank-fisheries of the Gulf of Mannar.

It is noteworthy that though their women do not now wear chank-bangles their children from four months to about two years old are often given roughly-made chank-bracelets to wear in the belief that such will protect them against the baleful influence of the evil eye, from vomiting and from a wasting disease called *chedi* which appears to be rickets and reputed to be caused by the touch or near approach of a woman during her menses! This custom has now been abandoned or is perfunctorily performed by some of the better class Parawas, but the great majority, including naturally the whole of the poorer and more ignorant sections of the community, continue to adhere strongly to the custom. The bangles are roughly fashioned and with the crudest of ornamentation; they are made by Muhammadans at Kilakarai, their chief settlement on the coast of the Gulf of Mannar.

Apart from this evidence we have nothing of importance till we come to the sixth century when the travelled monk, Cosmas Indico-Pleustes, after mentioning the island of Ceylon, proceeds to say " and then again *on the continent* and further back is Marallo which exports conch shells (*κοχλίους*)." Sir J. Emerson Tennent in his " Sketches of the Natural History of Ceylon " (London, 1861) misses the significance of the expression " on the continent " and identifies Marallo with Mantotte near Mannar on the north-west coast of Ceylon, where chanks are collected in the neighbourhood in large quantities even at the present day. Yule [1] with closer adherence to the old text would place this ancient chank-fishery on the Indian coast (*i.e.*, on the continent opposite Ceylon), and he suggests that Marallo is a corrupted form or misrendering of Marawar, the name of the chief caste living in the coastal district of Rāmnād, now the location of one of the most productive and accessible present day chank-fisheries. The name of the local people not infrequently was applied by old travellers to the chief town in their territory and so, very reasonably, we may identify Marallo generally with the Maravan coast and particularly with either the town of Rameswaram or of Pamban situated at the western extremity of Adam's Bridge and directly opposite to Mantotte and Mannar at the western extremity.

[1] *Cathay and the Way Thither*, Vol. I, p. clxxviii, London, 1866.

Ma'bar or Maabar, the Arab name for the western coast of the Pandyan country, has probably a parallel derivation, Maabar being indeed a very fair rendering by guttural Arab lips of the Tamil term Maravar.

The next writer to mention the chank is the Arab Abouzeyd, who in 851 A.D. stated that "they find on the shores of Ceylon the pearl and the shank, which serves for a trumpet and which is much sought after." [1]

A long gap occurs in references by travellers to chank-fisheries till the days of the Portuguese and Dutch when they became fairly frequent. A few years before the establishment of the former power in the Gulf of Mannar, the traveller Barbosa visited the old town of Kayal, and from him we learn that it was then still an important seaport where many ships from Malabar, Coromandel and Bengal resorted every year to trade with the rich Hindu and Muhammadan merchants living there, a definite statement which shows that there was even then no difficulty in forwarding supplies of chanks direct by sea to the Dacca workshops.

Barbosa also tells us that at the time of his visit the fishery off this coast belonged to the king of Koulam (Quilon in the southern part of Travancore) who generally resided at Kayal and who farmed the pearl-fishery to a wealthy Muhammadan.[2] The chank-fishery so far as we know has always been an adjunct to the more romantic pearl-fishery and must almost certainly have been treated in a similar manner, both fisheries being considered everywhere in India from immemorial times as prerogatives of the sovereign. About 1524, the Portuguese seized the Tinnevelly pearl-fishery, stationing a factor and guard boats on this coast—the Pescaria or fishery coast as it soon became termed. In 1563, Garcia da Orta speaks of the trade with Bengal having declined owing to the unrest caused by Muhammadan invaders in that country, but in 1644, Boccaro in a detailed report upon the Portuguese ports and settlements in India records that a large quantity of chanks fished off Tuticorin were exported to Bengal "where the blacks make of them bracelets for the arm." He adds rather quaintly the name of another Tuticorin production—"the biggest and best fowls in all these eastern parts." [3] Exactly how the Portuguese conducted this trade and what profits it yielded them are not known to me; the Dutch, so far as they were able, destroyed the Portuguese archives in Tuticorin as well as in Ceylon, and we must await further research among the records at Lisbon before we can gain any further information.

The Dutch, keen to distinguish the substance from the shadow, paid great attention to the development of the chank-fishery as distinguished from the pearl-fishery whereof one of their most able local Governors, Baron Van Imhoff, once queried (1740) whether the latter "is not more glitter than gold as so many things are which belong to the Company, which shine uncommonly but have no real substance." [4]

[1] *Fide* Yule's "Hobson-Jobson." [2] *Fide* Yule's "Hobson-Jobson," article "Chank."
[3] *Fide* Yule, "The Book of Ser Marco Polo," Vol. II, p. 307, London, 1871.
[4] Hornell, "Report to the Government of Madras on the Indian Pearl Fisheries in the Gulf of Mannar," Madras, 1905.

In 1700, Father Martin, a Jesuit Missionary, wrote (*Lettres Edifiantes*, II, p. 278, edition of 1843), " It is scarcely credible how jealous the Dutch are of this commerce. It is death to a native to sell them to any one but the servants of the Company. The shells are bought by the Dutch for a trifle, and then despatched to Bengal, where they are sold at great profit. These shells, which are round and hollow, are sawn and fashioned into bracelets equalling the most brilliant ivory in lustre. Those fished on this coast (Tinnevelly) are extraordinarily abundant; they have their spiral from right to left, but if one be found twisted in the other direction, it is a treasure valued by Hindus at an extravagant price, for they believe that it was in a chank of this description that one of their gods hid himself in order to escape the fury of enemies pursuing him in the sea."

With the transfer to the British of all Dutch ports on the Coromandel coast and in Ceylon together with the acquirement of the Tanjore and Carnatic territories about the same time, the control of all the chank-fisheries in these localities passed to the British.

The evidence furnished by the Tamil classics of the existence of an extensive chank-bangle industry in the extreme south of India during the height of ancient Tamil civilisation 1,200 to 2,000 years ago has received unexpectedly conclusive corroboration within the present year (1912) through discoveries which I have made on the sites of the once famous Tamil cities of Korkai and Kayal (now Palayakayal). These cities are now represented by mounds of rubbish adjacent to villages still bearing the appellation of their celebrated predecessors. The greatest find was at Korkai, which as already noted flourished from a date well antecedent to the Christian era down to some indeterminate date prior to 1000 A.D. when the accretion of silt at the mouth of the Tambraparni drove the inhabitants to build another city (Kayal) at the new mouth of the river. Here, on the landward outskirts of the village, I unearthed a fine series of chank workshop waste—seventeen fragments in all. The whole number were found lying on the surface of the ground in a place where old Pandyan coins have from time to time been discovered according to information gathered in the village. The fragments unearthed all bear distinct evidence of having been sawn by the same form of instrument, a thin-bladed iron saw, and in the same manner as that employed in Bengal at the present day. Eight fragments represent the obliquely cut " shoulder-piece," six consist of the columella and part of the oral extremity of the shell and the remaining three are fragments of the lips—all show a sawn surface, the positive sign of treatment by skilled artisans.

At Kayal or Palayakayal (*i.e.*, old Kayal) as it is now termed, the daughter city of Korkai, which flourished in the days of Marco Polo and appears to have grown rich as Korkai gradually passed away as a sea-port owing to physical changes in the delta of the Tambraparni, I found an excellently preserved sawn shoulder-piece, with marks of the apex having been hammered in after the present-day habit in Dacca workshops.

This was found on the surface in an open space within the present village. Time did not allow me to prosecute a detailed search, but in my own mind the single fragment found is conclusive evidence of the industry having once been located here. No shell cutting of any description is carried on anywhere in this neighbourhood.

Again, at Tuticorin, I have found a sawn and hammered shoulder-piece of typical form, hence as the three discoveries were all made at places which in turn have been the head-quarters of the chank-fishery, I am fully convinced that at all three, chank-bangle workshops formerly existed, to treat on the spot this product of the neighbouring sea. Why the seat of the bangle-cutting trade became transferred or limited to Bengal is obscure, and may never be satisfactorily elucidated ; I am, however, inclined to suggest the hypothesis that the decay of the industry in Tinnevelly may have been consequent upon the Muhammadan invasion. The date of the passing away of the chank-cutting industry I am inclined to put tentatively at about the fourteenth century, a time which marks the close of unchallenged Hindu supremacy in the south, the spoliation of the vast riches of the Pandyan cities by the Moslem and the heyday of Arab sea-power on this part of the Indian coast. With the depression and decay entailed by the loot and ruin of their enormously wealthy temples and long prosperous cities by the invaders under Malik Kafur and his lieutenants it is far from improbable that the particular trade here referred to became disorganised within the Pandyan realm and forced into a different channel, the whole of the shells being exported to Bengal to be cut there instead of being treated locally at the seat of the fishery.

It is also noteworthy that the huge funeral urns found in tumuli of the Tambraparni valley (at Adichanallur) have yielded a few fragments of working sections cut from chank shells, associated in the urns with beautifully formed bronze utensils, iron weapons and implements and gold fillets. So old are these tumuli that they are classed as prehistoric though it is obvious that the people of those days were skilful artizans in gold, bronze, and iron and must have been contemporaries of historic periods in the story of Egypt and Mesopotamia.

In this connection, as bearing upon the antiquity of the trade connections between India and Persia, some interesting exhibits are to be seen in the Louvre, Paris ; the most noteworthy is a chank-shell cup, probably used in libations, found by the Mission Dieulafoy in the ruins of Susa. It measures 6½ inches in length and has been longitudinally bisected a little to one side of the median line, the larger portion being retained to form the cup. The columella has been cut out and the result gives a very serviceable form of spouted cup. It is classed as of Achæmenid age—say *circa* 500 B.C. From the same ruins the Mission de Morgan brought back a fragment of a large chank bangle nearly one inch wide (No. A7532) roughly ground to a triangular ridge pattern in section and with a rough $<$ mark engraved at one side.

Again the Fouilles de Tello yielded to the Mission de Sarzec a number of perforated chank-shell fragments sometimes very finely engraved ; one in particular (No. 221) bears a spirited representation of a lion leaping upon the back of a bull. These objects were apparently ornaments worn suspended from a cord.

As there are no chank-fisheries in the Persian Gulf, these objects must have been imported from India either from Kathiawar or from the Gulf of Mannar. The libation cup would seem to show a much more widely spread use of the chank shell in ancient times than we have hitherto suspected and research directed to this special point in collections coming from Babylonian, Assyrian and ancient Persian sites should throw further light on this subject.

(b) THE FORMER EXISTENCE OF BANGLE FACTORIES IN THE DECCAN AND IN GUJARAT AND KATHIAWAR.

I have been unable to obtain any evidence from ancient Indian writings of the existence elsewhere than in the extreme south of the country of any ancient custom of wearing bangles cut from chank shells. Probably such references do exist, and if this be so, I trust the present notes may elicit their quotation by scholars who are familiar with the ancient Sanscrit and Gujarati classics, the most probable sources of information.

Fortunately, in this apparent absence of written records, archæology has important evidence to offer, and although it is difficult to date the greater portion of this testimony with any exactitude, it offers irrefutable proof that the industry of chank-cutting and the custom of wearing chank bangles had once much less restricted geographical range than at the present day.

Apart from the finds in the Pandyan country, mentioned above, a considerable amount of archæological evidence exists proving that extensive chank-bangle factories were located in ancient times in the Deccan and in Gujarat and Kathiawar. The principal finds proving this were made by the late Mr. Bruce Foote; they are now deposited in the Madras Museum and form an exhibit of wonderful and unique interest.

The remains obtained in these localities consist of two distinct series; one comprising fragments of finished chank-bangles which appear to have been once actually worn, and discarded owing to accidental breakage or else purposely broken as a sign of mourning, the second, either of sawn rings of chank shells—working sections—ready for the bangle carver and polisher or of waste material from chank-bangle cutters' workshops.

In the Southern Deccan and neighbourhood chank-bangle fragments have been found in the following districts and States, namely :—

Mysore.
Bellary.
Anantapur.
Kurnul.
Raichur Doab.
Guntur.
Kistna.

Careful examination of the museum collection leads me to believe that shell-bangle factories existed at four centres in the area indicated, the principal being :—

(1) Hampasagra on the Tungabhadra, Bellary District.
(2) Bastipad on the Hindri River, Kurnul District.
(3) Maski in the Raichur Doab (Hyderabad State);
and (4) at the great Buddhist ruins of Amaravati in Guntur District.

Of all these, the last named discovered by Mr. Rea, lately Archæologist to Government, is probably by far the most important, as we are better able to date the remains here than anywhere else owing to their association with buildings of known origin.

The chank fragments discovered at Amaravati are very numerous and important, giving evidence that the chank-bangle industry was carried on in this locality even earlier than the construction of the Buddhist buildings. They consist in the main of large numbers of fragments of working sections of the shell together with a very few pieces of finished and ornamented bangles. Besides these are numerous waste pieces—shoulder and oral rejects, showing that the methods of cutting up were identical with those of the present day. The whole of these fragments were found beneath the foundations of buildings which the most competent authorities date *circa* 200 B.C., hence these bangle fragments are antecedent thereto and must be over 2,100 years old. It may be that these remains constituted part of the town's rubbish heap before the erection of the Buddhist buildings which have survived to the present time and that this rubbish heap was employed in making or raising the ground prior to the putting in of the foundations, or it may be that an old village site, including the waste of a village bangle factory, was selected as a site by the Buddhist architects of Amaravati.

Besides bangle fragments, a few rudely carved chank finger-rings figure among the remains, together with small discs of $\frac{3}{4}$ inch diameter sometimes perforated in the centre; the latter were used in the fashioning of necklaces—at Peddamudiyam in Cuddapah, Mr. Rea has found complete necklaces formed of spherical chank beads alternating with chank-discs of the pattern here referred to. The perfectly circular outline of these small discs is remarkable.

The two fragments of chank bangles found in the Kistna District are probably of approximately the same age as those from Amaravati as they also were associated with Buddhist remains. The finds in all the other districts cannot be placed in time in spite of their frequent association with neolithic weapons and implements. Mr. Bruce Foote has indeed suggested that finely worked serrate and biserrate chert and agate flakes found in one place in association with bangle fragments were employed by neolithic man to saw through chank-shells and to fashion bangles therefrom. This I cannot accept.

GUJARAT AND KATHIAWAR.

Mr. Bruce Foote's labours prove that the custom of using chank bangles was widely spread and that chank-bangle factories were numerous in these two provinces in ancient times.

The finds which he records are as follows :—

In Kathiawar :—

(*a*) Damnagar, Amreli Prant. In the fields (presumably upon the surface) north of the camping tope at this town a great number of chank bangles in a fragmentary condition were found and of these 41 pieces are represented in the Museum collection. Three working fragments were also found at the same place, together with a couple of cowries, and a Trochus shell ground upon three sides. Associated were such neoliths as a basalt corncrusher, a bloodstone hammer and chert and agate cores.

(*b*) Babapur. At this village situated 13 miles westward of Amreli, the alluvium of the left bank of the Shitranji river yielded a large and important series of neolithic chert flakes, scrapers, slingstones, and cores in association with 13 fragments of finished chank bangles, together with two working fragments and part of the columella of a chank. Several of the flint flakes are worked upon one or both edges, and one of the bangle fragments exhibits a chaste design executed with considerable delicacy. The other bangles are of plain and crude design.

(*c*) Ambavalli. Seventy-one fragments of broken bangles from an old site at this place are represented in the Museum collection (Nos. 3622-1 to 65 and 81 to 89). Of these the greater number are ornamented by pattern grooving and many show an elaboration of design as great as those now manufactured in Bengal. The designs in many instances are precisely the same as those in vogue to-day.

Associated with these bangle fragments were numerous portions of sawn sections of chank-shells, constituting the rough working material required by the bangle carver ; 33 fragments are shown (Nos. 3622-63 to 65 and 90 to 119).

With the exception of a few unimportant potsherds the only other object of importance found at this site was a small iron knife with tang. No stone implements were discovered, and no information is given as to the precise conditions under which any of the exhibits were found ; presumably they lay on the surface of the ground examined.

(*d*) Sonnaria. Fragments of two chank bangles of simple pattern apparently found on the ground surface. A chert scraper comes from the same locality.

(*e*) Kodinar. On the surface of Mr. Foote's camping ground were found several sawn portions of chank-shell, two being shoulder slices such as are found in the wastage from a bangle workshop.

(*f*) Vālābhipur (the modern Walah). From the ruins of the ancient city Mr. Foote obtained a large and most interesting series of chank-bangle fragments, 62 in number. With them were a smaller number (7) of sawn working sections. A few marine shells (*Nerita, Nassa, Ostrea,* and *Conus*) were also found among the ruins.

In Gujarat —

(*a*) Sigam, on north bank of the Heran River. Five weathered sawn working sections of chanks are represented in the collection from this site. No finished remains of bangles were seen. The site yielded a variety of neolithic flakes and cores and two sandstone hammers or pestles. No indication is given of the precise mode of occurrence, but I conclude they were all surface finds.

(*b*) Kamrej, 12 miles north-east of Surat. The summit of a small islet in the Tapti river at this place yielded three sawn shoulder slices (workshop waste) of chank shells and a single fragment of finished bangle. The latter is remarkable for the peculiarity and elegance of its pattern, a broad and closely worked zig-zag groove such as I have never seen either among ancient bangle fragments or on any of the present-day productions of Bengal. With these chank remains were two fragments of sandstone hammers.

This site is notable as being on an islet in the Tapti river protected against assault by steep and almost inaccessible sides—a place very defensible and therefore an ideal place for the settlement of craftsmen.

(*c*) Mahuri, in Vijapur Taluk. From " an old site at the head of the gully system which cuts deep into the alluvium of the Sabarmati " at this place, a series of working sections and waste pieces of chank shell was found sufficiently numerous and varied to convince me, after examination of the fragments, that a bangle workshop undoubtedly existed here at a remote period. The presence of sawn waste associated with sawn working sections is conclusive.

Of completed bangles the remains found were few (8 are shown in the collection) but of these, three are of special interest on account of the elaboration of ornament exhibited. Two of these fragments are of broad bangles richly carved in patterns very closely approximate if indeed not identical with forms in use at the present day. The third fine example is a tiny fragment of the narrow form of bangle known as *churi* in Bengal, usually worn in sets of three on each wrist. The other fragments found are of simpler patterns.

An interesting associated find was that of a small " finial " carved out of shell, probably mother-of-pearl. It is identical in form with a mother-of-pearl nose-pendant now in use among the poorer castes in some country districts in Bengal. An example which I purchased in Eastern Bengal is carved from the shell of a river mussel (*Unio* sp.). From the alluvium at Mahuri whence the bangle fragments came, a few neolithic implements, chert flakes and scrapers principally, were unearthed, together with several noticeable pieces of pottery. Of the latter, one is of special importance as it affords some evidence better than the neoliths touching the age of the bangle factory once situated at this place. It is a small headless figure of a sacred bull, of polished earthenware, red externally and black within. Two garlands are indicated around the hump by means of rows of tiny impressed punctures and there can be little doubt that it is of early Brahmanical age.

(*a*) Kheralu. A single fragment of a sawn working section of chank shell was found on the surface of the loess at this place.

Eight sites can clearly be indicated as probable centres of the chank-bangle industry in Gujarat and Kathiawar, namely :—(*a*) Sigam, Hiran Valley, Baroda Prant, (*b*) Kamrej, on the Tapti, (*c*) Mahuri, on the left bank of the Sabarmati, Baroda State, with (*d*) Ambavalli, (*e*) Damnagar, (*f*) Kodinar, and (*g*) in and on the alluvium of the Shitranji river above Babapur, all four in Amreli Prant, Kathiawar, also (*h*) Vālābhipur in Vala State, Kathiawar. At all these places working fragments of chank shells have been found. The most important sites appear to have been those at Mahuri in Gujarat and Ambavalli and Vālābhipur in Kathiawar. The unworked sections and waste pieces of shells found at these three places are so numerous, and so characteristic in their form of stages in shell-bangle manufacture, that we are perforce compelled to admit these sites as having been in old times locations of important factories, a conclusion to which further weight is given by the discovery at each of these places of fragments of completed bangles, in many instances of highly decorated patterns. At Ambavalli and Vālābhipur fragments of finished bangles are especially plentiful ; the ornamentation is well executed and exhibits considerable taste, a high degree of skill, and undoubtedly the employment of effective tools of several sorts—saws, drills, and files. Iron is the only metal suitable for making tools fit for carving the extremely hard substance of chank shells and it is of the greatest interest and significance that at the Ambavalli site associated with the many fragments of worked and unworked chank circlets found there, an iron knife with a tang was discovered which from personal examination I am satisfied may well represent such a chank-saw as is to-day in common use in Bengal chank factories for cutting patterns upon the bangles.

From a consideration of the details given above a certain number of facts and conclusions of importance emerge, to wit :—

(*a*) In all cases the fragments of bangles and of chank shells appear to have been surface finds. In several cases this is definitely stated and in the remainder wherever no statement of horizon is given, the context points to a like provenance. From this it follows that association with neolithic artifacts in itself has little value or significance ; both neoliths and chank fragments are practically indestructible by atmospheric weathering agencies and their association may merely connote the fact that particular surface areas have suffered little or no denudation or change since neolithic times whereby the broken implements and discarded ornaments of a later age have mingled with those of an earlier one. Or it may be the result of the artifacts of different ages having been weathered out of different alluvial strata in such way that they come eventually to lie together at a lower level of the original ground or else in some newer river deposit into which floods may have rolled them.

(*b*) The facts already noted that all sections of chank shells, working pieces as well as wastage scraps, show cleanly sawn surfaces as verified by examination of the originals now in the Madras Museum, and that these surfaces show series of striae *often at two or more angles to one another*, are sufficient to negative the tentative suggestion made by Mr. Bruce Foote assigning a neolithic origin to the workmanship. Neither serrate nor biserrate chert flake saws however delicately made could possibly produce such cleanly sawn sections as we see represented in the collection. The aid of thin metal saws must be invoked and it is most significant that in two instances (Ambavalli in Kathiawar and Muski in the Raichur Doab) fragments of iron knives were found associated with the remnants of chank working sections. In several other cases (Srinivaspur in Mysore, Havaligi Hill in Anantapur, and Bastipad in Kurnul) pieces of iron slag were found in association.

As the working sections of chank shells retain visible evidence of being sawn by means of a metal (iron) saw and as iron fragments are frequently associated with them, the evidence is to me satisfactory that the age of the former cannot possibly be neolithic ; knowledge of the manufacture of iron into somewhat elaborate tools—saws, files, and drills—must have been possessed by the bangle makers. This would appear therefore to rule out the early iron age, when iron weapons and tools were of primitive design.

Incidentally this conclusion is likely to affect the estimate of age accorded to the potsherds so frequently associated with fragments of chank bangles and to render doubtful their identification as neolithic or even of early iron age.

(*c*) Three sites alone give other than negative evidence in regard to age. These are Gudivada in Kistna district, Vālābhipur in Kathiawar and Mahuri in Gujarat. The remains at the first named are indubitably Buddhistic while the occurrence of a figurine of a bull with a double garland round the hump points distinctly to an age when the adherents of Brahmanism were in the land holding in especial reverence Siva's sacred bull. Most important find of all was that made in the ruins of Vālābhipur, for the history of this old city is fairly well known ; the dates of many of the great events that happened there are on record and the descriptions of two Chinese Buddhist pilgrims who visited the city are extant. The story of Vālābhipur goes back some centuries before the Christian era and for long it was the seat of the Valabhis, a Rajput race, and the centre of their rule, till the middle of the eighth century when the last of the line was overthrown by Arab invaders from Sind. Valabhi was visited by the Chinese pilgrim, Hiuen Tsang, in the course of his fifteen years' sojourn in India (A.D. 630-645) and by I. Tsing in the succeeding century. Both pilgrims describe it as a large and flourishing city and a great centre of Buddhist learning, its streets and schools crowded with students. The reigning dynasty, themselves of the Brahman faith, appear to have been tolerant of Buddhism like many of their contemporaries. In Hiuen Tsang's days the latter religion was still followed by great numbers of the populace, especially in Orissa and Southern India; elsewhere Hinduism was rapidly becoming the popular religion and the mass of the people were of this faith when the last Valabhi dynasty ended.

As the chank is a religious symbol both to Hindus and to Buddhists, we may reasonably conclude that the remains of chank bangles found in Vālābhipur were made for the use of the women of the town and neighbourhood not later than the eighth century. The trade must have been long established at that time to judge by the excellence of the work turned out, which fully equals that of average Bengal workmanship of the present day.

Taking all facts into consideration I am inclined to date the majority of the bangle fragments found in the Kathiawar and Gujarat sites as roughly contemporary with the Vālābhipur specimens or at most not antedating them by more than 300 to 400 years.

To date the Deccan chank-bangle factories is more difficult; one outstanding fact is the simplicity of all the patterns. The great majority are devoid of ornament save for a boss roughly carved at one side. This plainness of design would seem to bespeak less skill on the part of the Deccan workman than on that of his fellow craftsman in Gujarat. If that be the explanation, and if it be not due to lack of taste or of the means to pay for good work on the part of the buyers, then we may reasonably date the majority of these fragments back to the first few centuries before or after the beginning of the Christian era. The presence among the pottery mixed with the bangle fragments found near Srinivaspur in Mysore of a flat sherd similar in pattern to one found with the Buddhist remains at Gudivada in Kistna District is noteworthy as lending further countenance to this conclusion.

(*d*) The finds made by Mr. Bruce Foote argue two great centres of chank-bangle manufacture and usage apart from that in the extreme south of the Madras Presidency, namely, one in the Southern Deccan and the other round the shores of the Gulf of Cambay. It is most probable that other centres of the industry did exist, but at present there is no direct evidence to this effect. For instance, it is not likely that an industry which was firmly established in Eastern Bengal at the time of the arrival of the Portuguese in India [1] and of Tavernier's travels in the seventeenth century, and which continues to flourish at the present day, should be of modern growth.

With regard to the third known seat of the industry in ancient times, that which flourished in the early centuries of the Christian era in the Tinnevelly district, its geographical location in the coastal section of the Pandyan kingdom made it the natural centre and home of a great chank-cutting industry. Its Pandyan sovereigns were from time immemorial overlords of the Pearl and Chank Fisheries of the Gulf of Mannar and

[1] Garcia da Orta writing in the sixteenth century states that the chank was then an article of importance in the Bengal trade, *though less valuable than formerly*.

Palk Bay, the most important source of supply of the raw material then and now, and it is a curious vagary of trade that the present seat of the industry should be situated 1,500 miles from the scene of the fishery.

From the fact that among a few widely separated castes, sub-castes and tribes of the extreme south of India, including among others the Kotas of the Nilgiri Hills and certain sections of the Vellalans and Idaiyans in the inland Coimbatore district, the custom prevails of wearing chank bangles for ceremonial reasons, we may also reasonably infer the former wider prevalence of the custom. Indeed it is probable that the custom was at one time prevalent throughout a large section of Southern India.

Kathiawar and adjacent Gujarat are also both maritime provinces and this geographical situation is the key to the location of a chank-bangle industry in those provinces in early times; the coast of Kathiawar is the only considerable source of chank shells apart from the Gulf of Mannar and Palk Bay. No chank-cutting is now done either in Kathiawar or Gujarat; the women there have abandoned their former habit of wearing chank bangles and all the shells fished in this locality are exported from Bombay to Bengal where they are known in trade as " Sūrti " shells, Surat having been the port of shipment prior to the rise of Bombay.

Why the Southern Deccan should once have been the home of a shell-cutting industry is not so easy of explanation, seeing that it is situated in the heart of the country and distant from 400 to 500 miles from the nearest sources of supply (Rameswaram and the Tanjore coast). Possibly the location of this trade in the Deccan was due to the superior skill as craftsmen of the people in this region inherited from stone-using ancestors who found in the quartzite and trap rocks of the district more suitable material for their weapons and tools than the men to the southward where intractable gneiss constitutes all the rocky outcrops. Certainly in prehistoric times, Bellary, Kurnul and Cuddapah were more thickly populated than the country to the south if we may judge from the evidence of the number of stone implements found respectively in these two sections of India. The neolithic remains of these Deccan craftsmen show their makers to have been comparatively highly-skilled workers and with the discovery of the use of iron, hæmatite ore being abundant in Bellary, the men of this district may reasonably be supposed to have developed special skill in the working of the new material into tools and in the manufacture of many articles, ornamental as well as useful, with the aid of these improved tools. Add to this the natural conservatism of tribes isolated from the coast by hill ranges—the customs and manners of the Deccan tribes have been less changed by contact and intermixture with surrounding races than the majority of the tribes or races living in the coastal plains. To these inland people the wonder of the great shell honoured by their gods would appeal vividly; the mystery to them of its origin would confer added importance and, as we find the wild hill tribes of Thibet, Assam, and Bhutan do at the present day, they would end by endowing ornaments made from it with mysterious powers of ensuring well-being and good luck, even as the

Buddhist cartmen of Ceylon and their Hindu brethren throughout the Southern Carnatic adorn their bulls with a chank shell as an amulet against the evil eye.

Chank shells for the Deccan bangle workshops may probably have come from the Tanjore coast, this being the nearest source of supply. The Tanjore fishery appears to have been fairly lucrative down to 1826 when economic changes caused a collapse of the industry. Tirumalavasal at the mouth of one of the northern branches of the Kaveri is the centre of the chank-fishery on this part of the coast and is not far from Kaveri-pattanam, once the chief port of the Chola kingdom and in the height of its prosperity in the early centuries of the Christian era. From Kaveri-pattanam to the inland districts of Kurnul and Bellary the transit of goods would be comparatively easy and safe ; coasters would be used to the mouth of the Kistna, 350 miles to the north, whence river craft would carry the goods direct to their destination, 200 miles inland. Or it may be that the shells required in the industry were fished further south, for we have mention by Cosmas Indico-Pleustes in the sixth century (*circa* 545) of a place called Marallo on the continent adjoining Ceylon, where a shell called by him κοχλίους (Kochlious) [1] was produced in quantity, and Yule in "Cathay and the Way Thither" (London, 1866), Vol. I, p. 81, suggests that this Marallo is the same word as Marawa, the name of the ruling caste in the district of Rāmnād ; if this be accepted, the reference would indicate the chank-fishery carried on off the coast of the Marawar country and now operated by lessees of the Raja of Rāmnād. Again, a chank fishery, the most productive in the world, exists to-day in the shallow seas in the neighbourhood of Jaffna in Ceylon and direct communication by means of large native craft having existed from time immemorial between the north of Ceylon and the port of Masulipatam, for centuries the eastern sea-gate of the Deccan, this fishery may have been drawn upon also to supply the needs of the latter locality.

The cause of the cessation of the chank industry in the Deccan, Gujarat, and Kathiawar is to be looked for in the constant strife which kept India in a welter of blood through the six centuries of Muhammadan dominance in the land. From the days of Mahmoud of Ghazni, the northern and central portions of India in particular were harried by successive waves of fanatic invaders sweeping down through the north-west passes, and from the thirteenth century onwards to the end of the seventeenth the story of India is that of an unceasing contest between Muhammadan and Hindu for power on the part of the former and for existence and religion on that of the latter. Well may certain old Hindu customs have disappeared ; during the worst periods when the intolerance of the conquerors was at its height, their influence was often exerted towards the suppression of Hindu customs and this, combined with the dislocation of trade consequent upon the general insecurity of the country and the frequent recurrence of raids and widespread warfare, may be considered the main reason for the decay of

[1] In the Norman-French dialect still spoken in Jersey and the other Channel islands, the common whelk (*Buccinum*), which is the European representative of the Eastern chank, is known as coqueluche !

the chank-bangle industry in the Deccan and Cambay provinces. A striking confirmation of this conclusion is afforded by Garcia da Orta, a Portuguese writer of the sixteenth century, whose colloquies on Indian drugs and simples have recently been translated by Sir Clements R. Markham (London, 1913). In the thirty-fifth colloquy this old physician remarks :—" There is another (shell) they call chanquo, of which they make boxes, tables, and counters, for though it is rough outside, inside it is very smooth and beautiful. This chank is an article of trade to Bengal, and used to be worth more than it is now. The large ones, which we call Buzios, go to Bengal and are worked up very beautifully, remaining very smooth and white. For this only a small quantity is used, the rest being wanted for bracelets and other ornaments. It was the custom in Bengal that no person of distinction who was a virgin could be corrupted unless she had bracelets of the chank shell on her arms.[1] After the arrival of the Patans this custom was neglected and the chank became cheaper in consequence. You see here a chess table at your service where you may see the chank when you like."

[1] Another translation renders this sentence rather differently, to wit :—"There was formerly a custom in Bengal that no virgin in honour and esteem could be corrupted unless it were by placing chank bracelets on her arms." Da Orta's statement refers really to the fact that an essential ceremony in a Bengali marriage consists in placing a chank bangle on each of the bride's wrists ; the marriage would not be formally valid if this were to be omitted.

V

THE SCOPE FOR DEVELOPMENT OF A SHELL-BANGLE INDUSTRY IN OKHAMANDAL

At the present day the Indian shell-bangle industry is limited to Bengal, where in Dacca, Calcutta, Nadia, and other centres it gives lucrative employment to large numbers of skilled artisans. How economically important it is as an art industry will be realised when we learn that the value of the raw material required ranges between 2 and 2½ lakhs of rupees per annum as given by the importers, an amount probably understated so considerably that it is quite safe to put the average actual value at 2½ lakhs. This is the wholesale value; the shells usually change hands twice before they reach the actual bangle-workers; in turn the latter sell their products to bangle merchants who distribute them to shopkeepers and peddlers throughout Bengal, Behar, Assam, Bhutan and Thibet. The value increases several times in this process of manufacture and distribution till it is certain that the final retail value of the products of this industry at a conservative estimate is considerably over 15 lakhs of rupees, or £100,000. From one shell an average of three wide bangles can be cut; the wholesale value of good shells may be taken at from 1 to 2 annas each, whereas the one and a half pair of bangles that one shell produces will be sold at anything from 9 annas to rupees 18 according to the amount of ornamentation. Certainly the three bangles yielded by one shell have an average retail value of not less than one rupee. On this basis the shells increase in value eight times on the import value if we take the latter at the high rate of 2 annas each.

The tools employed by the shell-cutters and gravers are of the simplest and most primitive description; they consist of heavy double-handled saws employed in sawing the circlets which constitute the working sections for the bangle carver (*vide* Pl. IV, Figs. 1 and 2) and of small handsaws (Pl. V, Figs. 1 and 2), bow-drills and files for smoothing and carving the patterns. No labour-saving devices are used; the tools with the exception of European-made files, are undoubtedly identical with those used 1,500 years ago, in particular the great saw—the most important of these tools—which is referred to in an ancient Tamil poem quoted on page 59.

The present concentration of the shell-bangle industry in Bengal is consequent

Fig. 1.—Sectioning chank shells in a Dacca workshop.

Fig. 2.—Sharpening a chank saw, Dacca.

Fig. 3.—Breaking away the remains of the septum from a sawn chank circle (working section).

Fig. 4.—Rubbing down the inner surface of a chank working section, Dinajpur, Bengal.

[Photographed by J. Hornell.]

Fig. 1.—Carving an incised pattern, Rangpur.

Fig. 2.—Sharpening an engraving saw, Dinajpur.

Fig. 3.—Forming a simple ridge pattern by rubbing down the sections on a stone, Rangpur, Bengal.

Fig. 4.—Rubbing down cinnabar to colour lacquer red, Dinajpur.

[Photographed by J. Hornell.]

Fig. 1.—Lacquering marriage bangles, Dinajpur.

Fig. 2.—Method of using rest when finishing off an inlaid lacquer bangle, Dinajpur.

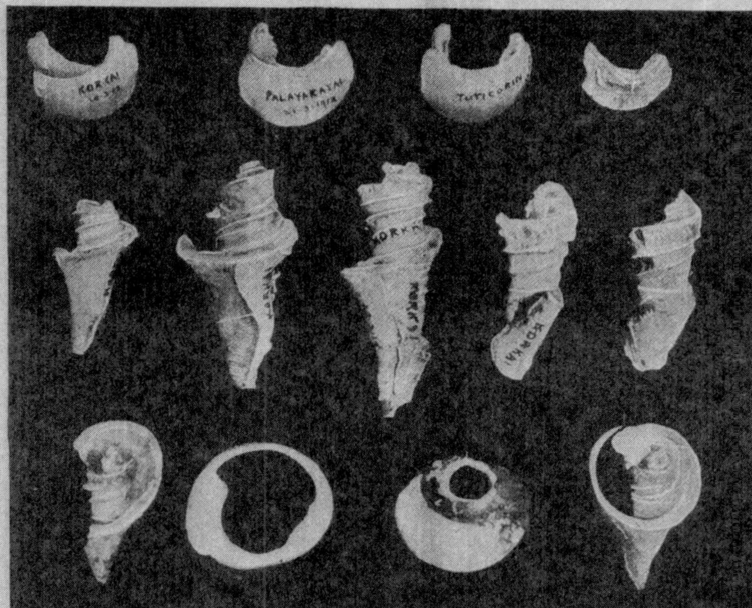

Fig. 3.—Chank shell waste from ancient bangle factory sites at Korkai, Kayal and Tuticorin (two upper rows) compared with modern waste pieces from Dacca (bottom row, where a working section is also shown).

Fig. 4.—Making children's feeding spouts from chank shells, Karimanal, near Pulicat, Madras.

[Photographed by J. Hornell.]

upon this province being the only one in India where shell bangles are extensively used by high and low among the female population. Even in Bengal itself shell-cutting proper—the sawing of the shells into working sections—is restricted to a very few centres ; this part of the work requires a great amount of skill such as can be acquired only after a long and toilsome apprenticeship, begun at an early age ; shell-slicing calls for the possession of a highly trained eye, perfect steadiness of hand and arm and an ironlike capacity to sit for long hours in a position of great discomfort. As a consequence the sawing of working sections is limited to a few centres and a good cutter is a valuable asset to his employer. To retain a hold upon these men, employers willingly give large advances in cash.

The towns and villages where the working sections are fashioned into the bangle patterns favoured locally are much more numerous than the sawing centres ; the bangle-workers in the great majority of such places do not attempt to slice the shell itself ; they depend upon the wholesale sawyers of Dacca and a few other great centres for their working sections. Particularly is this the case with Muhammadan bangle-workers, for these men are comparatively new recruits to the trade and therefore are employed chiefly in the less skilled sections of the industry and in fashioning bangles of the simple and crude patterns affected by the poorest and most ignorant of the population.

In spite of the two great advantages possessed by the bangle trade in Bengal—(*a*) location in the centre of the only province where chank-bangle wearing continues to be widely prevalent, and (*b*) the possession of a caste of highly skilled hereditary chank-bangle sawyers and carvers, there is ample scope for the establishment of a large chank-sawing industry in those localities where the shells are fished extensively—in Kathiawar and on the coast of the Gulf of Mannar. Indeed the proposition is one economically sound. At present the whole shell has to be transported from the place of fishing to Calcutta and Dacca, distances in both cases upwards of 1,200 miles, where the mouth part, the apex, and the columella, constituting over 60 per cent. of the total weight, are cut or broken away and thrown out as waste in the process of manufacture. Under present conditions freight and handling charges have thus to be paid on more than double the weight of the material actually employed. A radical change in the method of preparing working sections would, however, be necessitated as the present hand-sawing of the shell is an art too difficult for unskilled labour to acquire and I believe no Bengal sawyers would leave their own districts to work elsewhere. The one alternative is to adopt a form of machine saw capable of employment by comparatively unskilled workpeople. A band saw working with emery, or preferably with carborundum powder, probably would give satisfactory results, the motive power being either foot power leaving the hands free to hold and to guide the shell or, preferably, a small oil engine or else electric current in towns where the latter is available. The introduction of a chank-cutting industry into Okhamandal is, I believe, eminently feasible and practical and commercially sound. To begin with there is a considerable supply of shells available on the Okhamandal coast itself, and if this were to prove inadequate, it could be supplemented by supplies drawn from other parts of the coastline of Kathiawar.

The supply being therefore assured, the chank-sawing industry might be developed along either of two lines, either the shells might be sawn into working sections and these exported to Bengal in this partly manufactured state, or the finished bangle might be produced. With provision of a power machine suitable for cutting sections, this could readily be adapted to do smoothing, carving, and polishing, so that an intelligent workman —especially if he be one having some knowledge of lapidary work—if he were given a series of simple patterns to begin with and direction how to use the machine he has to handle, should have no insuperable difficulty in doing passable work in the course of a few weeks. Once he acquires a command over his machine and the ability to carve simple patterns, the power to attack more complicated patterns—such as those depicted on Plate VII—would soon come. As to a market, Bengal has now increased so greatly in population that the chank-bangle workers there begin to find difficulty in obtaining a sufficient supply of the raw material, so even if no local demand should develop in Okhamandal, the Bengal market would absorb readily all that an Okhamandal workshop would be likely to produce for years to come. It seems, extremely probable, however, that a more remunerative local demand may be counted upon to develop concurrently with the progress of the industry. Many thousands of pilgrims resort to the holy shrines of Bēt and Dwarka annually and these people, who value the chank shell as one of the emblems both of Vishnu and Krishna, as a vessel for use in their household religious ceremonies and, in many cases, as a curious souvenir of a memorable pilgrimage, would, I believe, esteem still more a handsome ornament made from this shell for their womenfolk, particularly if judicious efforts were made to draw attention to the appropriateness of such an ornament on the hands of Hindu ladies ; the beauty of its pattern, its snow-white colour—emblem of purity—and its general superiority to the gaudy glass bangles of European manufacture that not infrequently inflict serious wounds on the wrist when they are accidentally broken. Patriotic preference for a home-made ornament, especially when backed up by the more solid advantages of greater real beauty and greater strength and lasting property, should also count for much. Lastly, a most valuable potential market for high-priced chank bangles certainly exists in Bombay, Karachi, and other great cities where European and American tourists are to be found in yearly increasing numbers. These people are all eager to take home some "curiosities" of the East, preferably such as are not too bulky ; from my own knowledge I can say that well-carved chank bangles do appeal greatly to these visitors from abroad and it is only lack of enterprise on the part of Bengal chank bangle manufacturers that has prevented the exploitation of this promising field. Time after time people who have seen the chank bangles in my collection have expressed their desire to purchase—a desire baulked by the fact that none are to be had in any shops visited by tourists in any city in India.

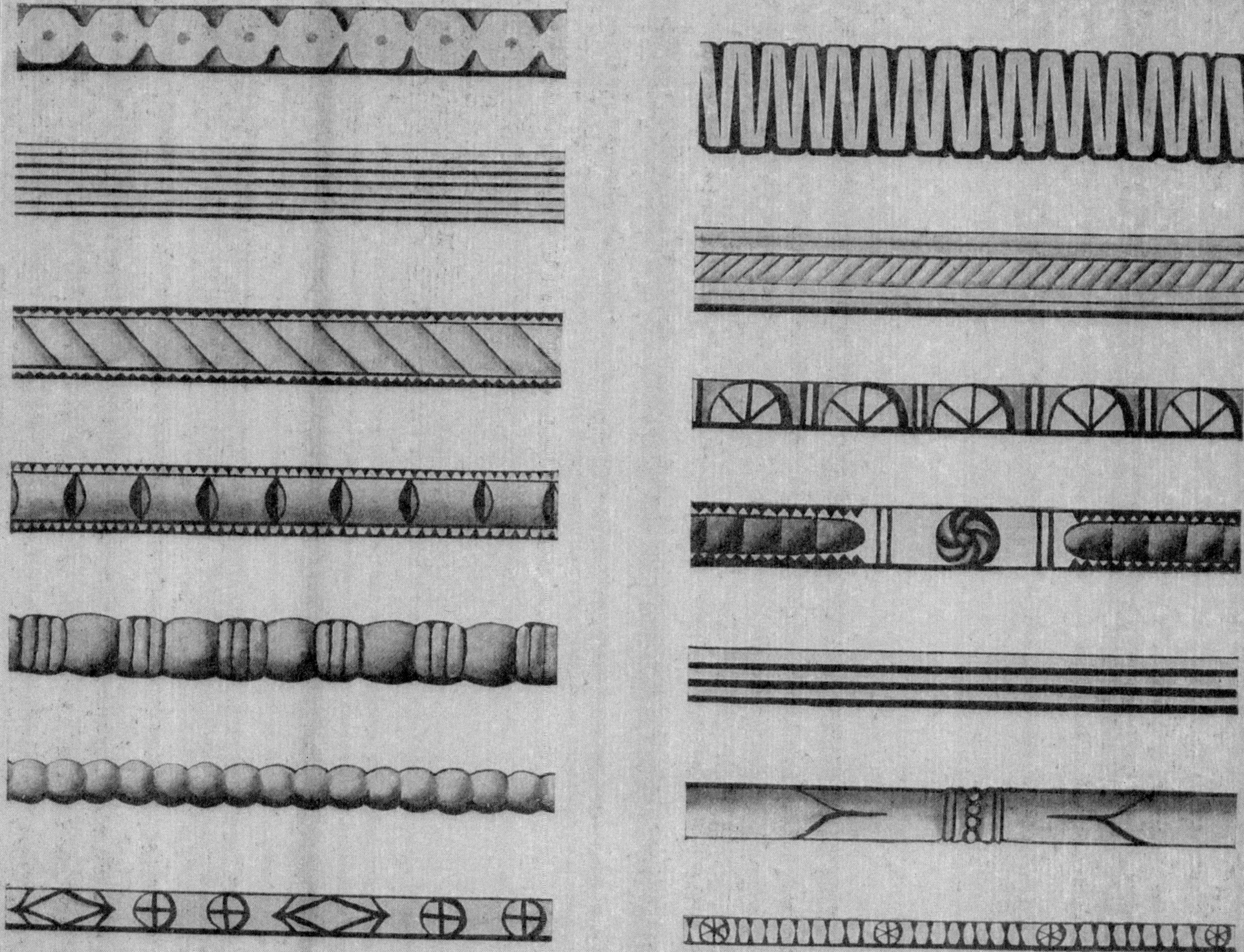

[Dorothy L. Hornell, del.

Pattern reconstructions of some ancient bangle fragments in the Foote Collection, Madras Museum.

Here, then, is an artistic industry requiring a minimum of capital to ensure handsome returns provided it be conducted with discrimination, enterprise, and honesty; well worthy of Government encouragement and of support by those who profess their desire to revive and develop the indigenous art industries of India.

At present the waste material produced when sawing bangle working-sections is not properly utilised. The bulk of it is burnt to produce lime, whereas much of it is capable of utilisation for button-making, seeing how great and increasing is the demand for buttons of an attractive appearance. In former days chank shell was also sometimes employed in inlaying; Garcia da Orta mentions the use of squares of chank shell in making the white squares of chess-boards.

EXPLANATION OF PLATES.

PLATE I (FRONTISPIECE).

Figs. 1, 2, and 3.—Sinistral chanks respectively in the Satya Bhamaji, Shank Narayan, and Lakshmi Temples, Bēt, Kathiawar.

PLATE II.

Figs. 1 and 2.—Immature chanks (*Turbinella pyrum*) from Okhamandal; both show persistence of the protoconch.

Fig 3.—Adult chank from Okhamandal.

Fig. 4.—Elongated variety from the Andaman Islands. Also two very young individuals with protoconch well shown.

PLATE III.

Fig. 1.—Group of Cheruman Women wearing necklaces of so-called chank-rings.

Fig. 2.—Under a banyan tree. Selling chank shells to pilgrims returning from Bēt.

PLATE IV.

Fig. 1.—Sectioning chank shells in a Dacca workshop.

Fig. 2.—Sharpening a chank saw, Dacca.

Fig. 3.—Breaking away the remains of the septum from a sawn chank circle (working section).

Fig. 4.—Rubbing down the inner surface of a working section, Dinajpur, Bengal.

PLATE V.

Fig. 1.—Carving an incised pattern, Rangpur.

Fig. 2.—Sharpening an engraving saw, Dinajpur.

Fig. 3.—Forming a simple ridge pattern by rubbing down the sections on a stone, Rangpur, Bengal.

Fig. 4.—Rubbing down Cinnabar (Hingol) to colour lacquer red, Dinajpur.

PLATE VI.

Fig. 1.—Lacquering marriage bangles, Dinajpur.

Fig. 2.—Rest used when finishing off an inlaid lacquer pattern, Dinajpur.

Fig. 3.—Chank-shell waste from ancient bangle factory sites at Korkai, Kayal and Tuticorin (two upper rows) compared with modern waste pieces from Dacca (bottom row, where a working section is also shown).

Fig. 4.—Making children's feeding spouts from chank shells, Karimanal, near Pulicat (Madras).

PLATE VII.

Pattern reconstruction of some of the ancient bangles in the Foote Collection, Madras Museum.

REFERENCES.

The two most frequently quoted works in this Report being :—

> Thurston, Edgar.—"The Castes and Tribes of South India," 7 Vols., Madras, 1909, and
> Risley, H. H.—"The Tribes and Castes of Bengal," 2 Vols., 1891,

references thereto are abbreviated to the author's name followed by the number of the volume and the page therein quoted, *e g.*, Thurston, II. p. 21.

PRINTED IN GREAT BRITAIN BY R. CLAY AND SONS, LTD., BRUNSWICK STREET, STAMFORD STREET, S.E., AND BUNGAY, SUFFOLK.